Echoes of Contempt

To all those whose stories I have heard
and to those who never got to tell theirs.

What does it matter if year after year passes and there is no end in sight to that road? Such is the fate of a Jew. If they drive him out of one place, he'll cower in another. If he runs away from there, he'll wander on. And wherever he happens to stop for a while and catch his breath during his flight, he sets up his temporary, shaky house that falls apart with the wind.

Bogdan Wojdowski
Survivor of the Warsaw Ghetto,
Bread for the Departed, 148

First, set fire to their synagogues or schools and cover with dirt whatever will not burn, so that no man will ever again see a stone or cinder of them.
Second, I advise that their houses also be razed and destroyed.
Third that their prayer books and Talmudic writings . . . be taken from them.
Fourth, that their rabbis be forbidden to teach henceforth on pain of loss of life and limb.
Fifth that safe conduct on the highways be abolished completely for the Jews.
Sixth, that . . . all cash and treasure of silver be taken from them.
Seventh, I commend putting a flail, an axe, a hoe, a spade, a distaff, or a spindle into the hands of young, strong Jews and Jewesses and letting them earn their bread in the sweat of their brow.

Martin Luther
The Jews and their Lies,
1543

His blood be on us and on our children.
Matthew 27:25

Contents

Acknowledgments — ix

Introduction — 1

Chapter 1
A Struggle for Hearts and Minds — 8

Chapter 2
A Hatred Defined — 22

Chapter 3
Darkening Times — 36

Chapter 4
Stigmatization and Segregation — 46

Chapter 5
From Reformation to Enlightenment — 61

Chapter 6
The Emergence of Race and State — 72

Chapter 7
Edging Closer to Catastrophe — 83

Chapter 8
"Of Course This Isn't Antisemitism" — 105

Bibliography — 125

Acknowledgments

A WISE MINISTER OF mature years, the Reverend Douglas Hubery, once said to me, "It doesn't matter whether it's new, what matters most is if it's true." He made this statement decades before fake news became an issue. What I have sought to do in this book is present the facts as I have received and understood them. Much of what I have written comes from the work of those far more gifted than I, therefore I have tried to ensure that every reference has been recorded. If I have missed any, I do apologize. I need to acknowledge first and foremost the tremendous amount of work others have undertaken over the years to attempt an understanding of the long, dark history of Judeophobia in the Christian church and elsewhere.

Then there are those who have directly influenced me through presentations I have attended and conversations I have had the privilege of taking part in. I am most indebted to two friends: Rabbi Brian Fox, who was at the time rabbi of Menorah Reform Synagogue in Manchester, England; and the Reverend Canon Albert Radcliffe, also of Manchester. It was they who first opened my eyes to the part the Christian church played in the persecution of Jews, the pogroms and the Holocaust.

Then of course there have been the survivors who somehow found the courage to share their deeply moving testimonies. The late Jan Fuchs provided insights that couldn't help but inspire. Gisela Feldman travelled with her family and nine hundred other Jewish refugees on the MS *St. Louis* to the far side of the Atlantic and was refused asylum. Her grace has touched me on each of the all-too-infrequent occasions we have met. Eva Schloss's seemingly-tireless drive to change the world through speaking tours is beyond compare. Her humor and her friendship consistently restores my faith in humanity. I have been truly blessed in life to have met such extraordinary people. They have impacted me and enlarged my views more than

Acknowledgements

they could have ever imagined. I pray that I can be worthy of their hope in continuing to ensure that the message is passed on.

Hosting the *Anne Frank and You* exhibition in 2006 and working with Gillian Walnes and her team drew me deeper into the roots of the Holocaust and made me even more aware of the warning signs in our own time. The Anne Frank Trust UK remains a special organization committed to building the world Anne envisaged.

In 2012 I was fortunate to attend a ten-day seminar for clergy at Yad Vashem, the World Holocaust Remembrance Center, thanks to the Council of Christians and Jews. The coordinator was Yiftach Meiri. To have sat at the feet of leading Holocaust academics, not least Professor Yehuda Bauer, was an experience I shall always deeply value.

In Britain the National Holocaust Centre and Museum is Beth Shalom, not far from where I now live. For more than two decades it has raised awareness of where prejudice leads and has nurtured thousands of school children and challenged adults. It has been a great privilege for me to come to know the Smith family (founders and inspirational educators) as friends.

A Christian challenging Judeophobia in the church can be very lonely. When I have put my head above the parapet and sought to challenge the Judeophobia of today, John Levy has been an ever-dependent listening ear and encouraging voice. John, whose father was Rabbi Isaac Levy, Chaplain to the British Army at Belsen, has been one in whom I could depend at such times. So too my loyal Methodist colleague and confidant, the Reverend Colin Smith.

For the last five years, lecturer Mark Plater has allowed me to inflict my musings on his BA History class at Bishop Grosseteste University in Lincoln, UK. This has allowed me to try and make sense of said musings in as accessible a manner as I could, so I am indebted to him.

Those who have helped me fine-tune this book include David Clitheroe and Dr. John Leonard. Their enthusiasm for the project has kept me going and their willingness to scrutinize the text has ensured it is better presented than it would otherwise have been.

It has been helpful to have my long-standing friend the Reverend Peter Grimwood showing interest in the project, thereby reminding me of the need to complete it whilst keeping my feet on the ground.

With her customary willingness, Alison McNish stepped in on those occasions when I didn't feel like typing anymore. Anne Montefiore very

Acknowledgments

kindly ensured my initial submission was good enough to attract attention with her generous and wise advice.

David and Robert have become more than my sons; they are now my mainstays, ensuring that my passions, great as they are in this area, do not go over the top. As they grow older and more expert in their own professional roles (teacher of Divinity and Senior Program Manager for the Council of Christians and Jews, respectively), I know that I can always rely on specialist knowledge at the end of a phone.

I am also indebted to Stephanie Hough of Wipf & Stock for spotting all the omissions in what I thought was my completed effort!

Last, but most important, my wife Karen has put up with me for many years and has exercised especial patience with me on this whole subject when it has threatened to overwhelm me. We both know how important it is to get the message across because the world, and in particular the church, cannot afford to let this hatred continue any longer.

Introduction

To BEGIN WRITING A book is often either an act of faith or folly. I would like to think that in this instance it is a case of both. For if my faith means anything then it should lead me onto paths that some are reluctant to take. That is why I have committed myself to setting down what I have learnt and what I have now come to believe, since I first became aware of the church's complicity in that most evil of crimes: the attempted eradication of an entire race.

Of course, with regards to the subject matter, many before me (and indeed far better qualified than I) have taken a similar course by creating works on this darkest of episodes in human history. It is right that an event of such magnitude should demand responses from the greatest minds and require all their effort in addressing it. Their productivity has resulted in an output that leads some to claim, not always with good intent, that there is now a whole industry dedicated to those fateful years, the lead-up to them, and the subsequent aftermath.

So what is the point of adding another volume to the shelves found in most bookshops with yet more words on what must be the most examined event of the last century?

When it first dawned on me that the Nazi regime could not have brought into being the Final Solution without the Christian church, I seemed to face a monumental task. Those new acquaintances who drew my attention to the church's culpability seemed to know so much about the subject that I felt as if I had somehow been kept in the dark. Yet the vast majority of people in the congregations I served, and indeed many of my clergy colleagues, apparently knew even less than I. It is perhaps still true to say that many congregants know next to nothing on the anti-Judaism within the Christian Scriptures and church tradition. It certainly wasn't anything I can recall being made aware of during my days at theological college when I trained for ordained ministry during the early 1980s. Seeking to build on my newfound awareness of what the church had done to Jewish communities over the ages left me daunted by the prospect of delving into what appeared to be weighty academic tomes; there didn't seem to be much entry-level material available that was relevant to my quest.

So setting out on this journey of discovery was not easy. After much effort and not a little time (almost twenty years) spent reading books, articles, and papers, watching documentaries, attending lectures, and most importantly, listening to the testimonies of those who have either passed from this life or are now becoming too frail to continue telling their stories for much longer, I have felt compelled to place fingers on keyboard. I do so with not a little fear and trepidation. Who am I to attempt an introduction to this tragic history? I am not an academic, but then there are plenty of treatises already available for the serious student. I am not Jewish, but I believe that a Christian rooted in the evangelical tradition should ask the questions I am about to pose. I am not many things but I am who I am: a person keen to know the truth evidenced by fact, and a minister who wants the church I gave my life to many years ago to face up to the contempt with which it has held its closest faith neighbors for far too long (almost two thousand years, in fact).

To expose and address such deeply-seated prejudice in a community that espouses the causes of justice, righteousness and love is no mean feat. There have been occasions when I have attempted to do so, and as a result had not a little hostility pointed in my direction. Sometimes the reaction of others has been justifiable because in my newfound passion for the subject and naiveté I haven't shown sufficient compassion, care and understanding to get the message across effectively.[1] Having said that, there are many who would prefer to ignore our history of hatred, others who would want to deny it with a vehemence that actually confirms its presence, and only a few, in my experience, who are prepared to look afresh at our past and learn from it. Yet it is our solemn responsibility to do so, for surely the very essence of becoming all that God intends us to be is only achieved through

---

1. Hannah Arendt quoted in Rittner, Smith, et al. *Holocaust and the Christian World*: "Comprehension does not mean denying the outrageous, deducing the unprecedented from precedents, or explaining phenomena by such analogies and generalities that the impact of reality and the shock of experience are no longer felt. It means, rather, examining and bearing consciously the burden which our century has placed on us—neither denying its existence nor submitting weakly to its weight. Comprehension in short, means the unpremeditated, attentive facing up to, and revisiting of, reality—whatever it may be."

Introduction

reflection, repentance, and renewal. To avoid such a process is to limit the possibility of being as fulfilled as we might otherwise be in our discipleship. To avoid doing so as a community of faith is tantamount to something more than neglect: it renders the movement that began amongst the synagogues and gatherings in Galilee at the hands of a young Jewish preacher, prophet, teacher, and healer incapable of realizing its true potential: in other words, its claimed God-given destiny. Until the church becomes willing to fully comprehend the impact its teaching and traditions have had upon Jews and the Jewish communities over the centuries, willing to acknowledge its failure to admit that when it faced its greatest challenge it was found wanting, and willing, as a consequence, to embrace the necessary changes, it will never succeed in being all that it should be.

Hence the faith and the foolhardiness with which I undertake the writing of this book. It is an attempt to address a profound and disturbing matter so often only addressed either in lecture halls of universities or by those willing to wade through weighty tomes in order to make some sense of their growing awareness of the church's failure. Of course, some have drawn upon the centuries-old contempt towards Jewish communities and the inaction, indifference and complicity in the Holocaust as an axe to wield against the church they already despise. As a consequence many within the church have chosen to ignore their attacks, believing them to be the result of ulterior motives. But we would do well to understand why it is that such views are held and what evidence there is to back up such views. Better still would be if we could come to the point of contrition. Yes, we have been predisposed to prejudice all along; yes, many of our Scriptures were written in such a way as to drive a wedge between us and the Jewish communities; yes, our history includes hatred toward those with whom we have more in common than the vast majority are prepared to admit; yes, we have justified appalling actions by recourse to warped theologies; yes, six million Jews were rounded up, transported, selected and executed by, in the main, baptised Christians; yes, we have failed to repent.

What now? The time has come, indeed it should have come long ago, for us to admit our mistakes. The lonely voices over the centuries that called us to examine our erroneous contempt have come and gone without eradicating the evil that has held our mission in abeyance; indeed its very presence has consequentially rendered our mission nigh on impossible. The time has come to look at what we have done in the name of God, a God who must surely weep at the suffering, weep with the expelled and tortured, and indeed weep over a church that has so much potential yet remains resistant to change.

On examining the history of the Christian church's attitude toward those who have resolutely held onto their faith during the most tortuous of trials and tribulations, it seems that Jews have never been able to escape the envy, suspicion and hostility heaped upon them.

Storytelling is a strong tradition within Jewish communities, from the tales that found their way into Scripture to the fables of Eastern Europe in recent centuries, or from novels to the film scripts of today. Many of the stories are parabolic in that they seek to tell a truth, offer some form of teaching, or make sense of a predicament, and predicaments are not an uncommon feature of Jewish life. Some of those stories try to explain why they are so persecuted.

One such story is of a community of mice that act upon the words of the "Advisor," one of their own. When asked for the reason why the cat hunted them down, the Advisor noted that all troubles stem from hatred and hatred arises out of jealousy; the reason for the cat's jealousy is obvious, he said: the mice sport such nice, long tails. Therefore there is only one course of action that the Advisor believes will rid the mice of persecution at the claws of the cat, and that is to trim their tails; it will be painful but it will be worthwhile, for by doing so the cat will no longer be jealous and their problems will be over. One old and wise mouse suggested they approach the cat and ask for his help, because tearing or biting off their own tails would be very painful, but the cat might do them a service and be persuaded to carry out the task for them. With his pointy, sharp teeth he'd slice through the tails without much effort and hopefully without prolonged agony for the mice. Some of the other mice also believed that the move would be sensible in that everyone knows one has to kowtow to the wicked and flatter them. Sadly it didn't quite work out how the Advisor or the old and wise mouse had intended; for a cat is still a cat and whether mice have long tails or none, they are still mice.[2]

The fable was composed by Romanian Eliezer Shtaynbarg during the early part of the twentieth century in the face of ongoing pogroms and before the rise of the Nazi threat. It clearly exposes us to the despair many Jews feel, that no matter what actions they take to avoid the age-old hostility against them, they will still be persecuted and hunted down.

---

2. Shtaynbarg, *The Jewish Book of Fables*, 3–5.

Introduction

Here is another story from later in the century. It is an imaginary episode that only Jews could tell with such irony. Hitler is at the podium ranting and raving at the difficulties Germany is facing, lamenting defeat in the Great War, lambasting the Versailles Treaty that unjustly punished Germany, reminding the audience of the catastrophic economic collapse, and stating that "we all know who is to blame."

At this point, Moshe at the back pipes up: "The cyclists."

The hall falls silent, Hitler scans the sea of faces and asks, "Who?"

"The cyclists, Herr Fuehrer," repeated Moshe.

Hitler is perplexed. "Why the cyclists?"

And Moshe concludes "Why the Jews?"

Why indeed.

Such a sense of fate has evolved over centuries and is entirely understandable even to those who have taken the briefest of glances at the history of Jews in their relationship with non-Jews. The question "Why the Jews?" is the critical one we need to address and in so doing we will come to better appreciate the role of the church. There are well-argued excuses for two thousand years of church contempt towards Jews and they are unedifying to say the least. Our task is to examine them, put them into their context, and consider how they have impacted upon others and brought discredit to the church. It is a tall order. Addressing centuries of false teaching, hateful preaching and misguided beliefs doesn't come easily or quickly but it is something we must do if we are to hold our heads high without the arrogant bigotry that has punctuated our history. I would prefer to hang my head in shame than to hold it high without recourse to confession and repentance.

Despite my best efforts to avoid making mistakes there will no doubt be some within this text. They are entirely innocent and I apologize in advance for not spotting them. There are certainly omissions; this is after all only a brief introduction to a vast subject, and particular aspects are addressed far more comprehensively by others. I am convinced that some will criticize me for including or leaving out what I have, perhaps finding it unpalatable or even biased. By doing so they could well be overlooking the possibility that they merely confirm my argument that any perspective other than their own is invalid. This would not come as a surprise to me, as I have grown accustomed to being attacked for exposing what I believe to be truths long overlooked; nor will it be a surprise for anyone who reads this book with care, compassion, and openness. For we shall see that the history of the Christian church is littered with those who have preferred to not address their inherited prejudice when it came to taking up a position either for or against the Jews.

Before we go any further I must offer a word on terminology. In recent decades the term *antisemitism* has become the preferred choice to describe all prejudice against Jews. This is understandably so because the darkest episode in human history, the Holocaust, had at its core racial prejudice against Jews. Nazi ideology did not differentiate between those who practiced Judaism faithfully and those who chose not to. Even those whose grandparents had become baptised Christians decades before were forced into the cattle trucks to the camps. Racial prejudice against Jews is known as *antisemitism*. Sometimes we will see the term written as anti-Semitism; to do so is to assume there is such a thing as Semitism: there is not. For example, Zionism is a political view, and since it exists, so too does anti-Zionism. But there being no such thing as Semitism means that a more accurate way of writing racial prejudice against Jews is *antisemitism*. Such prejudice only came to the fore in the mid-to-late nineteenth century as interest grew in race, ethnicity, or nation of birth. Prior to that, and for pretty much eighteen centuries, the predominant reason for hostility toward Jews tended to have a theological basis. Yes, there would be envy, suspicion, and fear, but these were fueled by a religious prejudice fostered by the Christian church. A better definition of this form of prejudice is *anti-Judaism*. In more recent times, especially since the founding of the modern State of Israel in 1948, a new form of hostility bearing the hallmarks of past prejudice has taken hold. This political prejudice is best termed *anti-Zionism*. All of this will become much clearer as the book progresses. For me, one term captures the whole gamut of Jew-hatred and that is *Judeophobia*.

Lastly, it is important for us to consider another term that has a hold over the public imagination. The *Holocaust* has come to be seen as the all-encompassing action against Jews across Nazi-occupied Europe, whether that be the events of Kristallnacht on the night of November 9, 1938, the mass killing of Jews in the forests of conquered Soviet states, or the gas chambers of Auschwitz. There are some issues with using this term, chief among them being that it has come to be used to describe other events, such as the genocide of other races elsewhere and at other times. Indeed, some may even use the term *environmental holocaust* to describe the impact of humanity on the planet. To use the term *holocaust* for anything other than the attempt to eradicate Jewry by Nazis and their accomplices in the middle

Introduction

years of the last century takes something of its uniqueness away.[3] The term preferred by many is *Shoah* which is Hebrew for *catastrophe*. This seems far more appropriate. I would choose to use this term when conversing with Jews or with those who have given much time to studying the events of those years. But it is still a long way off from being in common usage. As a consequence and for ease of access, I have elected to stick with the term *Holocaust* in this book. However, the reader might note my frequent use of the term *catastrophe* when forlornly attempting to describe the tragedy that was to engulf European Jewry.

Whether my effort to produce an accessible account of these past two thousand years of Judeophobia comes to be viewed as an act of faith or folly is for others to judge. My sincere hope is that some will gracefully accept it as a sincere contribution to correcting a long-standing wrong within the Christian church. In the relatively early days of Christianity, St. Augustine of Hippo (354–450) repeated the lie that Jews had killed Jesus and went on to liken them to Cain who had killed his brother Abel. According to Augustine, as with Cain, Jews were to wander the earth destitute as a form of punishment. We shall conclude by considering the possibility that for two thousand years Christians have been persecuting and killing their sibling Jews and have in fact become Cain to their Abel.

---

3. But the term itself isn't wholly appropriate especially to many Jewish scholars. "Holocaust" is Greek for a sacrificial or burnt offering as in that Abraham was to have offered Isaac up as a "holocaust." No matter how common the use of the term Holocaust is today, we can surely all agree that the Final Solution was neither a sacrifice nor a burnt offering but a catastrophe of epic proportions.

Chapter 1

A Struggle for Hearts and Minds

History is written by the winner. This is so true. At the end of the Second World War, British Prime Minister Winston Churchill was told that Field Marshall Alan Brooke (later First Viscount Alanbrooke), Chief of the Imperial General Staff, was penning an account of the war and that it would probably not show the Prime Minister in an entirely favorable light. Churchill is said to have responded by claiming that history would show him in a good light because he would write that history. As indeed he did with his six-volume version that easily outstripped sales of Alanbrooke's account.

But it's not only history that is written by the winner: theology is too.

We may think that there is a myriad of traditions in the Christian world today, but virtually all of them in the West have their roots in the movement that was begun by Paul and a small number of his companions. Similarly so with contemporary Judaism: there may be a number of forms today, but they all arose from the embers of the burning Temple that left only Pharisaic Judaism viable. It was these two expressions of faith battling for the hearts and minds of Jews and those attracted to the Abrahamic faith that would help foster the environment in which centuries of conflict would ensue. However, these two groups, Pauline Christianity and Pharisaic Judaism, were not the sole representatives of their respective faiths during the first century, far from it; like today's denominations, they were each just one of many.

With the passing of time, interpretations would overlay the original debates between Christianity and Judaism in the first century, leaving a conundrum for those seeking to understand what was actually being said. The easier option was to believe that the perspectives expressed by the writers were an accurate reflection of the reality; in other words that their prejudices were true. Such a course of action has not only been disloyal to the texts upon which the opinions have been formed but also a disaster on all sorts of levels: lies have been told, intercommunity relations have suffered, lives have been lost, and whole ways of being that had been forged over centuries have been wiped out forever.

The real loser has been the one both Christians and Jews claim to serve, and in the collective responsibility sense, the Christian church must shoulder much of the blame. The sins of our spiritual ancestors have been visited upon us whenever we have fallen for the false teaching over the previous centuries.

It comes as a great shock to many within the church to be told that the Holocaust could not have been undertaken without centuries of uncorrected prejudices based on the teaching and traditions of a church which in turn had their catalyst in the books of the Christian Scriptures (New Testament) and the writings of the early church. It is a shock, but a necessary one to address if we are to overcome the views that led to the mass graves at Babi Yar and the gas chambers of Auschwitz-Birkenau. If we don't face this fact, then the claim "never again" will continue to fall on deaf ears.

When the temple finally fell to the legions of Titus in 70 CE, after the Zealots had occupied it for four years, it seemed that much of Judaism was lost with it. Surely its traditions, beliefs, and religious festivals could only be diminished or destroyed by the fact that the once physical focus of the faith was now in ruins. Indeed the event ranked alongside the fall of Jerusalem six centuries previously when in 586 or 587 BCE (the date is disputed due to conflicting calendars and documents) the city was sacked, Solomon's temple was razed to the ground, and the elite were taken into captivity in Babylon. However, just as the Babylonian Exile was not only a disaster but also a time of soul searching, eventually leading to a renewed understanding of what it was to be the People of God, so the destruction of Herod's temple gave rise to fresh thinking. Out of the ashes arose a new form of the religion that was not necessarily bound to the old ways. The Judaism from the time of Jesus no longer existed, but, as we shall see later, it served the purposes of the church to claim that it did.

The strand of Judaism that survived the onslaught in 70 CE was Pharisaic Judaism. For generations of readers of the Christian Scriptures, especially Matthew's account of the gospel but not exclusively so, this could mean only one thing: the "enemies of Jesus" had survived. Jesus had battled long and hard against that *"brood of vipers,"* as John the Baptist would reputedly call them.[1] Subsequent commentators and preachers would heap further hostility on the heads of the Pharisees. They did so whilst choosing to overlook the hints contained within Luke's account that suggested the Pharisees weren't that bad a bunch. Had they not hosted Jesus at meals? Had they not warned Jesus that Herod was out to get him[2]? But the overriding view in the Christian church of Pharisees, and to a certain degree to this day, was one of hostility, with the 23rd chapter of Matthew's account being the foundational document for such contempt. Hypocrisy, spiritual blindness, cheating, lying, and a fair few other allegations are laid at the door of the Jews, claims that would resurface again and again in the centuries to come as Christians described the activities and character of Jews; after all, "who can trust a Jew?" It is no coincidence that the compiler of Matthew's account should place this tirade immediately before claiming that Jesus foresees the destruction of the temple. As we shall see shortly, the document was put together in the days following the destruction of the temple, and at that time only the Pharisees had remained an effective competitor for the hearts and minds of the people. There would have been no need for the gospel accounts to dismiss the Sadducees, Essenes, or any one of the other sects within Judaism as forcefully, as these were no longer a threat to the emerging movement.

The survival of Pharisaism is a fascinating one. The story goes that Johanan ben Zakai, a leading Pharisee of the time, pleaded with the Zealots to negotiate a peace with the besieging Roman forces. When he found them bent on fighting to the last, he managed to secrete himself out of the city in a coffin carried by his disciples. Once beyond the Roman lines he sought a negotiated settlement with Vespasian, the father of the commanding officer of the Roman forces, Titus. Predicting that the temple would be destroyed (even without the benefit of hindsight there would have been no great surprise there) and that Vespasian would one day become Emperor, Johanan found favor and secured support for his movement. He clearly knew how to make friends and influence people. Johanan turned his school at Yavneh (or Jamnia), near the Mediterranean coast, into the center of Jewish studies. It was here that the implications for Judaism would be debated

1. Matt 3:7.
2. Luke 13:31.

in the aftermath of the temple's destruction. During this time the matter of atonement without a temple was worked through, where prayer replaced animal sacrifice and Jewish Messianism was fostered. It's not difficult to see how close all of this was to the developing theology of the first Christians: a trusted leader, who appeared to be dead, went on to create a strong and attractive movement that no longer depended on the temple or animal sacrifice. Both movements came to conclude that the manner in which a life was conducted determined whether the relationship with God was healthy or not.

It must have appeared to some followers of Jesus, especially those that had held on to their Jewish roots, that Pharisaism was indeed coming to similar conclusions regarding the faith and ethics of Judaism but without reference to Jesus. It was at this time that the gospel according to Matthew was compiled and the clash between the two movements is evident throughout many of its chapters. But the relationship hadn't always been so strained. It is probable that any arguments between Jesus and other teachers were little other than the norm for their day, since religious debate was, and still is, the stuff of Judaism. Visit any *yeshiva*, where Jews study religious texts, and you will find plenty of lively debate. It is sometimes said, by Jews I hasten to add (any Jewish story I recount has to have been told to me by a Jew), that if you put two Jews in a room you get three opinions. It was surely no different at the time of Jesus. Debates on the meaning of life and how atonement could be achieved were not a pastime or form of entertainment; they were about nothing less than life and death. Satisfying God was the most important feature of life: not only was the health of the individual dependent on it but so too was the welfare of the community and security of the nation.

Because of what was at stake, various expressions of Judaism were present at the time of Jesus. We have already referred to the Pharisees, and the gospel accounts tell us that there were also scribes. The scribes were closely associated with the Pharisees in that they too were anxious to interpret the Law in ways that affected the manner in which people conducted their day-to-day lives. But not all Pharisees were scribes; hence the classification found in the Christian Scriptures.

We also know something of the Sadducees. For example, unlike the Pharisees, the Sadducees did not believe in a life after death. In not holding such a belief it could be concluded that their teaching was that much further removed from the teaching of Jesus. Their views therefore impinged less than the Pharisees' on the Jesus movement. So even though they are not painted in a positive light by the gospel accounts, they seem to get away with less hostility directed at them. Of course their way of life, often coming from the upper echelons of society, may have been close to anathema to Jesus, who was charged with associating himself with those on the margins of society. Therefore the Sadducees were probably so beyond the sphere of activity of the early followers of Jesus that they were seen as less of a threat. Another reason for the Sadducees being seen by the church as a lesser rival than the Pharisees was the fact that they had rejected oral tradition. Both Jesus and the Pharisees vied for truth and an ethical behavior based on traditions that had emerged outside the written texts.[3]

Another sect, but one that is not mentioned in the New Testament possibly because of their complete extinction after the fall of Jerusalem, were the Essenes. Now known more widely because of their monastic-style community in Qumran where the so-called Dead Sea Scrolls were found between 1946 and 1956, the Essenes held interesting views, some of which seem to have influenced aspects of the Christian church. Indeed their "Teacher of Righteousness," the one that they were waiting for, seems to bear some striking similarities with Jesus. Their teaching has a degree of resonance with the teaching of Jesus and the early church. Some have argued that Jesus himself may have been an Essene. This is unlikely because he accepted the hospitality of those whom the Essenes considered unclean and therefore were anxious to avoid. However, it is possible that Jesus may have been influenced by the Essene community with its belief that the "Teacher of Righteousness" would soon arrive and God's new kingdom would be ushered in. It is as interesting, if not more so, to reflect on the possibility that John the Baptist may have been an Essene. His geographical sphere of activity was not far removed from the Qumran site and his lifestyle, like that of the Essenes, was frugal. Like the Essenes (and Jesus) John did not view the temple as being the place where atonement with God could solely be found.

We also know of another group at the time of Jesus, namely the Zealots. Some of the first followers of Jesus, including named disciples no less, belonged to this politicized form of Judaism. Simon was one of the Twelve yet we are not told anything about him except that he was a Zealot. Why could that be? Is it something to do with the Zealots being in conflict with the Romans? They were, after all, the freedom fighters of their day, bent on

---

3. Reuther, *Faith and Fratricide*, 65.

overthrowing the occupiers and restoring the fortunes of Israel by force. Later, the early church were anxious to keep in with the rulers, especially when those rulers happened to be Roman. It may not have been helpful to draw too much attention to the fact that Jesus had chosen Zealots to be amongst his most trusted group. The question as to whether Judas was a Zealot or not is still debated. If he is known as Judas Iscariot what does the latter half of his title tell us? Some scholars argue that Iscariot comes from *Sicarii*, a particular group within the Zealots that carried small daggers known as *sicae*. Others have argued that Judas may have come from Kerioth, a small Judean town and that therefore he was known as the "Judean from Kerioth," Judas Iscariot. If the latter explanation is accurate it may have put him at odds with the other members of the Twelve who were from "up north," the Galilee. This, alongside other factors as we shall see later, was to play a part in helping foster further suspicion and hatred of Jews at intervals over the centuries.

And what of the Baptizers? The followers of John the Baptist are often overlooked as a significant force in their own right, yet they existed long after John's death as far afield as Corinth.[4] Indeed, the lengths to which those New Testament writers would go to ensure that John is seen in a lesser light than Jesus begs the question: how great a threat to the early Christians were the Baptizers? In Matthew's account John is said to have described himself as not being fit to carry the sandals of the one who was to come, and that John was reluctant to baptize Jesus because Jesus should have been baptizing him.[5] When he is imprisoned John sends his disciples to Jesus to ask if he was the one whose coming had been foretold.[6]

Then there were the Jews of the diaspora. These believers were scattered all around the known world. They would have been more influenced by Hellenistic teaching and other philosophies than those Jews settled in the biblical land of Israel. Amongst them would have been converts who may never have set foot in Jerusalem, let alone the temple; as a consequence their attachment to it was minimal. They were therefore ripe for attraction to movements that had little or no allegiance to the temple such as Pharisaism and early Christianity.

These groups within Judaism did not cease to exist at the end of the earthly life of Jesus. It is therefore no exaggeration to say that after the

---

4. Acts 19:3.
5. Matt 3.
6. Matt 11:2.

crucifixion and before the fall of the temple, the early followers of Jesus were just one of many groups existing within Judaism. For much of that time the relationship wasn't as strained as it was to become in the following centuries. But the writing was on the wall. This is evidenced by the writings of the New Testament, in particular the gospel accounts, which grew in increasing hostility as each new version was produced.

Mark's account was the earliest and was mainly composed, with a few later additions, prior to the destruction of the temple. It tends to dwell on the passion and crucifixion of Jesus. Matthew's account was written after the destruction of the temple, and because of the struggle for hearts and minds noted above, seems preoccupied with the opposition of the Pharisees to Jesus.[7] It can be argued that as Christian theology developed so too did a form of prejudice that we can term as nothing less than anti-Judaism. By the time we get to John's account, possibly produced well into the second century, the anti-Judaism is rife.

For those raised from childhood in the teachings and practices of the Christian church, where anti-Judaism is so well established through a non-critical approach to Scripture, one that avoids understanding the context and where a theology targets an entire people, it becomes a huge challenge for one to see little other than the false claim that Jews failed to heed the teaching of their own prophets, rejected Jesus, and had him killed. For many with a post-Auschwitz mind, this is deeply disturbing. But there are plenty who still find it difficult to make the link between what was written so long ago with the events of more recent decades. This is undoubtedly in part due to the fact that Scripture is still so revered that the reasons for its particular take on the events cannot be questioned; it is after all, "gospel truth." The truth is: not quite.

A gap between the followers of Jesus and other Jews was present throughout the ministry of Jesus and beyond. We have already seen that Judaism, like any major faith, was not a homogeneous unit of belief. Jesus and his disciples, all Jews, explored the boundaries of their faith in conversation with their contemporaries as well as with ancient texts and traditions. Judaism itself, in its many forms, was not immune to outside influence, nor would Christianity be in the years that followed. But after the death of Jesus and the claim that Jesus was somehow resurrected, the debate deepened. It would be inaccurate to claim that the followers broke from Judaism at this point. But it has been, and in many quarters still is, a commonly-held view

---

7. Abel, *The Roots of Antisemitism*, 112.

that at the resurrection, or on the day of Pentecost just fifty days later, a whole new religion came into being: one that divided the followers of Jesus from those Jews that continued to reject him.

For decades, if not for centuries in certain communities, the relationship between the followers of Jesus and those that held on to other forms of Judaism remained fairly strong. It is not possible to identify a moment when Christianity broke from Judaism because it simply didn't happen like that. Differences of opinion grew and divisions opened up at periodic intervals in the diverse places where the early church existed. It is of course naïve to use the Christian Scriptures as the sole source for the history of the first century church. It is not accurate to suggest that only one form of Christianity existed. Different expressions of the new faith evolved in various ways in relation to the belief systems and cultures in the vicinities in which it found itself. Much of it was, for the first few decades and in some places for a very long time after one of Judaism's many sects.

The activities of Paul and the dispute as to how far gentiles had to be Judaized before they could be admitted to the community of believers was little other than a reflection of the debates found within a proselytizing Judaism of the time. Today we are familiar with the fact that the vast majority of Jews are born into the faith and that converting to Judaism is a difficult and drawn-out process; but this is only as a consequence of what took place centuries later. We shall see later that it was the Christian church and the Christian rulers that would ban conversion to Judaism. At the time of Jesus and in the following decades it was not unusual to convert to Judaism. Whilst it is a turning point in the development of the early church, the debate between Paul and Peter in Jerusalem over circumcision and dietary laws[8] was little more than a dispute between first-century Jews. Neither Paul nor Peter would claim to have abandoned Judaism even if they were practicing it differently. Indeed many followers of Jesus would continue to uphold Jewish Law and practices, celebrating the festivals and honoring the Jewish Sabbath. For many, Jesus had come to reform Judaism, not to create a whole new religion. But the problem for Paul, and for those who were engaged in a similar mission to his, was the increasing numbers of converts to the faith who had little or no desire to ascribe to Judaism. When gentile followers of Jesus began to outnumber Jewish followers in cities such as

---

8. Acts 15.

Antioch, Jewish rites began to lose their popularity and necessity in the eyes of the followers so that they ended up being practiced rarely, if at all.[9]

The early followers of Jesus were a diverse bunch. Their beliefs and practices were far from uniform. But at least many of them were operating alongside, and at times within, an understanding of Judaism. However, events would ensure that the communities would continue to diverge. This was so after the Great Fire of Rome in 64 CE and the cataclysmic events in Jerusalem just a few years later. It was then that the gospel accounts came to be compiled and written in such ways that ensured a gap between Judaism and what came to be known as Christianity. It was a gap that would rarely, if at all, be bridged again.

But before we go any further it might be wise to reflect upon the fact that a number of claims have already been made. We have already noted the existence of many different groups and sects within Judaism at the time of Jesus: Pharisees, Sadducees, Zealots, Essenes and Baptizers. There were almost certainly others for whom little if any evidence exists as well as subgroups within the ones we have already mentioned. Many rabbis would have their own particular emphases with their own disciples, such as the Galilean Hanina ben Dosa, a younger contemporary of Jesus. Hanina was said to be able to cure the sick, even at a distance; therefore the similarities with Jesus are plain to see. Likewise the earlier Honi the Circle-Drawer was reputed to be able to stop or bring on rain at his command.[10] But the similarity between Honi and Jesus doesn't stop with having a command of weather conditions, for Honi was also killed in Jerusalem at Passover.

It could be argued that the intention of Jesus was not to create a whole new religion but to forge a new group within Judaism, or in other words a movement not dissimilar in relationship to the rest of Judaism as that which existed for other groups. After all, Jesus is said to have come for the benefit of the lost sheep of Israel.[11] As we have already highlighted, but shall do so with greater force shortly, it would suit the purposes of the early church to use this view to condemn contemporary Jews in their alleged unwillingness to accept the teaching and will of God. Other texts will remind us of the reluctance of Jesus to break away from Judaism, but as we shall see, this only served to reinforce the view that other Jews, by their actions and unbelief, forced the schism. Jesus had come not to abolish the Law or the prophets

---

9. Abel, *The Roots of Antisemitism*, 128.
10. Vermes, *Jesus in His Jewish Context*, 127.
11. Matt 15:24.

but to fulfil them.[12] His instructions to the disciples included the directive to not bother with the gentiles but to those within Israel who needed to be reminded of their duties and brought back into the flock.[13] The gospel accounts would later refer to the disbelief of his coreligionists as a reason for the wholesale rejection of Judaism and the embracing of a brand new religion. Over the centuries this claim would develop. Not only was Judaism no longer seen to be the route to God, but it was the path to hell; all Jews, not only contemporary to Jesus but for all time, would be responsible for the death of Jesus and therefore judged in this life and hereafter.[14]

There is little doubt that the death of Jesus was a catastrophic event for Judaism in that interpretations of its meaning would be used as an indictment against Jews. Understandably the Jews were to continue lamenting firstly the fall of Jerusalem in the sixth century BCE and their subsequent exile, secondly the destruction of the temple in 70 CE and the estimated killing of thousands of Jews, and thirdly the cataclysmic Simon bar Kochba revolt of 132–136 CE, which had a profound impact upon Jewish history as control of Jerusalem was lost to the Jewish nation for almost two millennia. But it could be argued that the crucifixion of Jesus would have as great an impact upon Jews, with generations of Christians using it as a pretext for persecution and pogrom. The unjustifiable claim made by many Christians that Jews were responsible for the death of Jesus grew with time. It became deeply embedded within the theology of the church and the mind-set of its members. No such claim can be found in the letters of Paul or in the early sources that would be drawn upon by the gospel writers. By the time the accounts of Matthew and John came to be compiled, however, the blame appeared to be firmly laid at the door of Jews: not just those who happened to have been in the city at the time, nor those few who may have actually had some hand in the arrest, trials, and judgment, but all Jews everywhere and for all time. "His blood be on us and on our children"[15] records Matthew as Pilate expresses his desire to be free of the guilt that may come to be associated with the death of Jesus. This verse is a blatant attempt to justify attacks on Jews, and could be paraphrased, "they brought it on themselves, Governor." Later, John's account would be even more vociferous: Jews were

12. Matt 5:17.
13. Matt 10:5–42.
14. Matt 27:25.
15. Matt 27:25.

said to be of the devil[16] and it was the Jews who clamored for the death of Jesus[17] whilst the synoptic accounts, Matthew, Mark and Luke referred only to crowds, chief priests, or scribes. One text that highlights how far removed the target audience for John's account had become from the actual events, and how great the gap now was between the Christians and the Jewish community is found in the record of one resurrection appearance when the disciples are behind locked doors "for fear of the Jews",[18] as if the disciples themselves were not Jews. It is sometimes claimed by those who wish to soften this blatant anti-Jewish terminology that John was merely abbreviating the term "Judean" to "Jew," and there may be some mileage in this, bearing in mind the fact that all the disciples, bar perhaps Judas, were Galilean. However, the term Jew (*Ioudaioi*) appears no less than 71 times in John's account, far more frequently than any of the synoptics.[19] It is clear that when John continually refers to expulsions from the synagogue the writer is referring to events not contemporary to Jesus but evident in the time of his own community. So the break with Judaism was well underway by the end of the first century when John's account was compiled.

It becomes a challenge for the preacher to have such knowledge and yet deliver a sermon that is not only faithful to the Good News but also of integrity. One writer who has provided a wonderful guidance in this is Marilyn Salmon who in her book *Preaching Without Contempt*, examines the anti-Judaism of the New Testament.[20] Once aware of the historical events surrounding the compilation of the gospel accounts and the reasons why each has its own particular emphases, Christian preachers can be more honest and therefore effective with their congregations.

As well as being written to ensure that the Jesus-event was written down for future generations, the Gospels were produced as a means for making a point. This was inevitable, if lamentable, as a consequence of what took place in the decades following the death of Jesus. Why hadn't all the Jews recognised Jesus as Messiah and come over to the new movement? Why had Jesus been put to death? Why had Jerusalem been destroyed?

As already noted, the Great Fire of Rome in 64 CE was one event that precipitated a change in the relationship between Jews and Christians. Nero,

16. John 8:44.
17. John 18:28–19:16.
18. John 20:19.
19. Salmon, *Preaching without Contempt*, 110.
20. Salmon, *Preaching without Contempt*, 110.

never one to accept responsibility for his own misdemeanors and incompetency, laid the blame for the destruction at the door of the Christians, and persecution ensued. Scholars have long taught that Mark's account of the gospel probably contains the reminiscences of Peter with Mark acting as scribe to the ageing apostle in Rome. Before the account was completed Peter was put to death during the great persecution, and out of necessity the early church in Rome sought to placate their rulers to avoid even further trials. So whilst Mark understandably emphasizes the virtues of martyrdom he also begins to shift the responsibility for the execution of Jesus from the Romans towards the Jews and indeed their reluctance to accept him as Messiah. Mark's gospel is the earliest known account of the trial that gives any detail. It describes Pilate believing that the high priests were simply jealous of Jesus and therefore offered the crowd the opportunity to free Jesus. There appears to be no historical basis for such a tradition so it may have been a ploy invented by Mark to placate the Roman rulers. Even when the crowd chooses instead to free Barabbas, Pilate asks them what he should do with Jesus and it is they who pass the sentence of crucifixion. The die was cast.

While Mark was writing in Rome the Jewish leaders in Jerusalem took little interest in the growth of Christian community.[21] Indeed there is evidence to suggest that relationships between the Jews and the followers of Jesus in Jerusalem were good at that time. James, the brother of Jesus, possibly the author of the canonical letter, and leader of the early Jewish Christian community in Jerusalem, remained faithful to Jewish practices. His story is one that is so often overlooked because of the emphasis within the Christian Scriptures on Paul and Peter. Robert Eisenman claimed that James and not Peter was the true successor to Jesus in the leadership.[22] James exercised a great influence over the believers and was held with high respect by his fellow Jews. Eusebius records that Pharisees went to James and pleaded that he get the followers of Jesus to tone down their views as it was causing a stir; James declined and when he was put to death (in 62 CE according to Josephus) some Pharisees pleaded for his life to be spared as he was a just man.[23] The Jewish Christian community in Jerusalem had lost their leader and quite possibly their last link to the earthly Jesus. Eight years later, Jerusalem fell to the Romans and members of that community were either dispersed or killed. The gentile church founded by Paul and his

21. Abel, *The Roots of Antisemitism*, 131.
22. Eisenman, *James the Brother of Jesus*, 7.
23. Painter, *Just James*, 128.

associates therefore became the dominant movement. As a consequence, James and his contribution to the growth of the movement was all but lost. The history of the church is, like other forms of history, written by the winners.

The First Jewish-Roman War of 66–70 CE, with the destruction of the temple as the climax, would set in motion further divergence between the followers of Jesus and rabbinic Judaism thus creating parallel movements. As we have already noted, the remnants of Judaism were scattered and the Pharisaic tradition under Johanan Ben Zakai would reform Judaism and eventually flourish. But the conflict between them and the followers of Jesus would grow. Anxious to continue their observation of Jewish practices, the surviving Jewish Christians persisted in synagogue attendance but their fellow Jews would insist on identifying them as different. A prayer was added to the eighteen daily benedictions, one which Jewish Christians were unable to recite as it called for the *minim* (Jewish Christians) to perish and be blotted out of the book of life; by this Jewish Christians were immediately identified and excluded from the synagogue.[24]

It was in the light of this worsening relationship, as Pharisees and Christians battled for the hearts and minds of the survivors of the Jewish-Roman War, that Matthew's account of the gospel came to be compiled. Matthew's account is the most Jewish of the four canonical gospels; it owes much to Pharisaism yet at the same time is the most hostile account toward the Pharisees. According to Matthew, the debates which Jesus engaged in were one of great intensity when Pharisees were involved. It is therefore reasonable to believe that Matthew put a degree of spin into the conversations making them far more confrontational than may have actually been the case. Even John fails to use the term "their synagogue" whereas Matthew uses it no less than five times and Luke once, showing that the expulsion may well have been either an ongoing or recent development in the experience of Matthew.[25] Each evangelist has his own reasons to identify the ones that are at fault. For Mark, due to the situation in Rome, the Jewish leaders were to blame and not the Roman forces. For Matthew it was the Pharisees, the only religious community that survived the destruction of the temple and which posed the greatest threat to the growth of the Christian community in his context. So the blindness of Judaism's teachers in Mark becomes for Matthew the blindness of the Pharisees.

---

24. Abel, *The Roots of Antisemitism*, 131.
25. Abel, *The Roots of Antisemitism*, 131.

The third Synoptic Gospel, the account according to Luke, was written at a time and in a place where the split between Judaism and Christianity was clearly evident and indeed deeper. By then it was not the religious leaders of the Jews, or a particular group within Judaism such as the Pharisees that were at fault, but the whole Jewish people. Luke and his contemporaries were keen to be seen as a gentile movement so as to avoid being judged as subversives within Judaism. According to Luke, Pilate is even more "innocent" than he is in Mark or Matthew, so much so that even his friend Herod cannot pass judgment on Jesus.[26] In compiling the Acts of the Apostles Luke would use the speech of Stephen before the high priest[27] to emphasize the view that Israel had forever been unfaithful, always grumbling about Moses and constantly rejecting the Law. The account is little other than a statement of the early church on its understanding of the failure of Judaism. The conclusion was that the Jews were stiff-necked, stubbornly proud, and though circumcised in the flesh had little to show for the covenant in their hearts. It doesn't get much clearer than that.

We have already referred to the heightened anti-Judaism of John's account of the gospel which was more developed than in the synoptics. For John, the church had now superseded the synagogue and was the "True Israel:" Judaism was past its "best before" date. By then Judaism was no longer seen by the church to be a valid biblical religion. Judaism and Christianity were now very distinct from each other. They had once battled for the same hearts and minds but one had become a winner in its own eyes and the other a loser. The historical record had been set down, but there was a lot more to come.

---

26. Abel, *The Roots of Antisemitism*, 134.

27. Acts 7.

Chapter 2

A Hatred Defined

IT IS OFTEN SAID that those who do not learn history are doomed to repeat it. A number of people have been credited with being the first to say so. The Spanish philosopher George Santayana (1863–1952) is popularly thought to have the edge on other claimants. In its original form the sentence read, "Those who cannot remember the past are condemned to repeat it." Whether history actually repeats itself is questionable. It is probably more accurate to suggest that events tend to rhyme or echo with the past. No situation in the course of history can be repeated exactly, but what does happen is that similar mistakes are made or an outcome could bear a strong resemblance to something in the past. Tuchman's Law[1] states: "The fact of being reported multiplies the apparent extent of any deplorable event by five to tenfold." The fact that an event is on record can make it appear to be continuous.

    Nevertheless there is sufficient evidence to suggest that history does tend to echo across the valleys of time. Again, it might be reasonable to claim that theology too echoes across the ages and indeed in those who live out that theology through their actions.

    In the decades after the destruction of the Temple in 70 CE and the founding of early Christian and post-temple Pharisaic communities, the seeds that had been flung to the wind began to locate minds in which to take root and germinate. Some seeds were good and some were not so good. Over the next few centuries the early church grew rapidly, and it's this growth that Christians have tended to promote and celebrate. But it

---

1. Barbara Tuchman, American historian, 1912–1989.

was also a time when the Jesus-movement went from being a sect of Judaism to its most vicious opponent. This is utterly ironic in that Christianity had been born within Judaism, the faith it sought to supersede. Indeed the church greatly benefited not just from the spiritual inheritance but also because proselytizing-Jews across the Empire had laid the groundwork for the new mission about to be undertaken by the followers of Jesus. Those who had been converted to Judaism were likely to be more receptive to the message conveyed by the followers of Jesus. These Jews had less interest in Jerusalem as a focal point for their faith and were therefore more receptive to a new expression of faith based on the traditions with which they were familiar.[2]

The consequences were catastrophic. Theologies were developed that tragically remained the bedrock of many warped views across the ages. The beliefs that were constructed out of ignorance and arrogance in those early communities were passed on from generation to generation and became the staple diet of preachers for centuries. The Christian church should have taken a long hard look at its hostility towards Jews, and on occasions it did, but it generally failed to do so for reasons we shall consider later. Lessons were consistently missed and we must now, in the dark shadow of the Holocaust and rising Judeophobia, ask if the present is but an echo of our distant past. Revisiting that past will provide for us a greater understanding of our spiritual ancestors. It will also help us to begin addressing the ongoing contempt with which we have held, and indeed many continue to hold, our brothers and sisters in Judaism.

Hostility on the part of the Christian church towards Jews in those early centuries was such common currency that the term "Jew" came to be used to describe anyone with whom the church was in dispute. In other words, not only were those that upheld a Jewish faith Jews but also those who were not deemed to be "orthodox" Christians according to the prevailing beliefs of the time. Indeed Origen (185–252) would call those Christians that resisted the state "Zealots" and those that didn't hold to his particular theology "Pharisees."[3] This makes it a challenge for historians as they seek to discern whether the rhetoric employed by the authors of texts and sermons was directed at actual Jews or towards anyone they wished to slander. Interestingly, some Christian leaders would traduce church

---

2. Lazare, *Antisemitism: Its History and Causes*, 29.
3. Nirenberg, *Anti-Judaism*, 108.

communities when they were not being criticized enough by the Jews.[4] So the test of a faithful Christian included being criticized by Jews! However, that is just part of the story; there is so much evidence to convict the early church of anti-Judaism that we can be overwhelmed by it. There is little or no defence; few in the church sought to bring a case that presented the actual Jews in a decent light while many stood with the prosecutor no matter how unjust the court.

As we noted in the previous chapter, identifying when the church finally broke from the synagogue is not possible. It is true to say that even after the fall of Jerusalem, when the Pharisees relocated their center to Yavne on the Mediterranean coast and the Jewish Christians to Pella in modern-day Jordan, a fairly strong and viable Christian community continued to exist that related well to those within "mainstream" Judaism. In other words, some Jews who had accepted Jesus as Messiah remained close to the practices and beliefs of others within Judaism. It is equally true to say that these Jewish Christians, upholding the Torah and celebrating the Jewish festivals, remained in existence for centuries.

Many of the Christian communities elsewhere in the Roman world that had rejected Judaism came to know less and less of the existence of Jewish Christians, let alone interact with them. It therefore became easy, though deeply regrettable, for the gentile Christians to slander all things Jewish including those Jewish Christians who had held on to the view that Jesus was a reforming Jew, wanting to fulfil and not to abolish the Law. So whilst the "winners," those gentile Christians whose spiritual descendants thrived and whose writings tended to survive, composed their hostile views of Judaism and the ascendancy of the church, the "losers," Jewish Christians elsewhere in the world, were much more amenable towards Judaism. Sadly, the latter did not prevail. They were caught between a rock and a hard place; according to gentile Christians the Jewish Christians were too loyal to Judaism and according to Jews they were apostates. But Jewish Christians held on, especially so in Roman Palestine. They remained convinced that their Jewish neighbors would one day recognize that Jesus was indeed the Messiah, especially so after the temple was destroyed in 70 CE; the claim that Jesus foretold such a disaster only served to strengthen their conviction. But another revolt in 132–135 CE would put an end to such hopes for the most part.

---

4. Nirenberg, *Anti-Judaism*, 93.

When Simon bar Kochba, the leader of the rebellion in 132–135 CE, was proclaimed by the influential Rabbi Akiva (50–137) to be the Messiah, many Jews believed him. Their dreams were dashed in the defeat and utter destruction of Jerusalem at the hands of the Roman forces. As a consequence, surviving Jews became less receptive to the possibility of a saving Messiah; they were subdued for decades if not centuries to come.[5] The Jewish Christians in the region also suffered as no Jew was permitted thereafter to enter the city and the first non-Jewish bishop was appointed head of the Jerusalem church.[6]

Nevertheless, late second-century Christian chroniclers were still able to note the presence of a number of Jewish Christian sects, but this wasn't merely to record their existence: it was to highlight their heresy and the need for them to be "corrected." In the eyes of the writers these "heretics" were so close to Judaism that they were deemed to be "Jews." At least one writer, the Christian chronicler Hegesippus (110–180) based in Jerusalem, would go so far as to suggest that all heresies arose out of false Jewish teachings, irrespective of their actual source. This was particularly damaging as it was later claimed by Eusebius (260–340) that Hegesippus was a convert from Judaism. Gentile Christians, with little or no real understanding of Judaism, saw no reason for embracing a religion whose members had failed to recognize their own Messiah. Therefore any attempts by Christians to attach their faith or remain attached to the Jewish Law and festivals were seen as heretical. Those who condemned such moves could always turn to Paul and find in his writings conveniently harsh words, such as: "if anyone proclaims a gospel contrary to what you received, let the one be accursed!"[7] Time and again the letters of Paul and other manuscripts, not least those accounts that would become the canonical gospels, would be used as weapons to beat those with different viewpoints, irrespective of the fact that the same method could be adopted to put a contrary argument; this lesson has to be learnt in every generation, but sadly not always successfully.

Understandably, much of the argument surrounded the person of Jesus: was he wholly human, or wholly divine, or mysteriously both at the same time? This would be a long, drawn-out process and some might argue never solved adequately. It's a complex debate; it involves the matter of the death of Jesus, because how could the Messiah suffer the indignity

---

5. Parkes, *The Conflict of the Church and the Synagogue*, 115.
6. Parkes, *The Conflict of the Church and the Synagogue*, 93.
7. Gal 1:9.

of crucifixion? We may be familiar with the "proof texts," drawing on the prophets, especially Isaiah, to "prove" that the Messiah was to be a suffering servant, but at the time the conclusions were not so easy to reach. The Jewish Christians were most likely to find it difficult to accept that Jesus was anything other than a human being. Many gentile Christians, accustomed to pagan gods coming to earth, had little difficulty in thinking of Jesus as God. The clash was inevitable and the hostility less than forgiving.

In order to cope with the vast store of Jewish Scriptures, Judaism's history, and its claim to be the chosen people of God, the early church began to disassociate itself from those traditions. Christian writers reviewed those texts and many argued that the covenant had been broken as early as the moment at Sinai when the Israelites were described by the Lord as a "stiff-necked people" (Exod 32:9), and the centuries thereafter were little other than a long, drawn-out divorce. In their judgment the history of Israel was one of unfaithfulness and punishment for the golden calf, through the rejection of the prophets up to the crucifixion itself. The destruction of the temple was clear evidence of God's anger and final punishment. The Jews were no longer Israel, because their Messiah had come and had been rejected, so they had been replaced by the church. The church alone was the "New Israel." Indeed some writers of the time would argue that Christianity had been present centuries before the Christ came to earth, in both Moses and the prophets. This view held that Jesus of Nazareth merely fulfilled the faithfulness of God's servants in previous generations, but like them he too was rejected by a godless people. Taking possession of Jewish heroes by the church as if they were its own was another nail in the coffin for the relationship between Jews and Christians. If Christ was the "Word of God," then he would indeed have been present throughout time, from the very beginning through the call of Abraham, the flight from Egypt, Sinai, and so on. It was claimed that God's people of those times were not Jews per se but a group within known as Hebrews and it was the Hebrews that had remained faithful to God, just as the Christians would do following the death and resurrection of Jesus.[8] The fault lay with the Jews. According to the early church fathers, Israel had never engaged in a single virtuous act ever.[9] The church has had difficulty shaking off such views since they were first promoted; the consequences have had the most horrendous impact. The arrogance of some today continues to ensure that such beliefs are not far

---

8. Nirenberg, *Anti-Judaism*, 102.

9. Parkes, *The Conflict of the Church and the Synagogue*, 158.

below the surface. James Parkes in his seminal work *The Conflict of Church and Synagogue* (published in 1934) sums up the catastrophe:

> "No people has ever paid so high a price for the greatness of its own religious leaders, and for the outspoken courage with which they held up an ideal and denounced whatever seemed to come short of it. If they had known the use that was made of their writings, then, indeed, many of the prophets might have obeyed literally the sarcasm of Irenaeus when he says that 'the Jews, had they been cognizant of our future existence, and that we should use these proofs from the Scriptures which declare that all other nations will inherit eternal life, but that they who boast themselves as being the house of Jacob are disinherited from the grace of God, would never have hesitated themselves to burn their own Scriptures.'"[10]

What became known as the Old Testament (itself a term designed to disparage it) would prove to be a "vast quarry," to use the term adopted by James Parkes.[11] Early Christian writers worked their way through texts to make some sense of the Jesus-event. Many ancient prophecies not at all related to Jesus would be used to "prove" that the views of these early Christian writers were correct. In order to get some idea of the gap between the words of Isaiah and other prophets and the events in Jerusalem at the time of Jesus, it might be useful to remind ourselves that the same number of centuries separate us from the signing of the Magna Carta. Such an understanding would not, indeed could not, have been accepted by those early Christian writers. Christian theology has ever since struggled to overcome such a mistake and many in the church still prefer ignorance of the context to an unpalatable truth. Cyprian (200–258), the bishop of Carthage, produced a list of no less than seven hundred texts to help preachers win an argument![12] The hijacking of the Jewish (or Hebrew) Scriptures would take to another level the deterioration of the relationship between Judaism and Christianity. The irony was that the church would use the Septuagint, a Greek translation of the Hebrew Scriptures riddled with errors, as its sacred book and use it to make its claims about Jesus, while the Jews would be castigated by the church for their inadequacies despite drawing on a more accurate text.

---

10. Parkes, *The Conflict of the Church and the Synagogue*, 106.
11. Parkes, *The Conflict of the Church and the Synagogue*, 99.
12. Parkes, *The Conflict of the Church and the Synagogue*, 100.

One of the prime protagonists of anti-Judaism in the Christian church was Origen (185–254), whom we mentioned earlier. He railed against the Jews for tolerating gentiles who worshipped idols yet also raged against Christians with "insatiable fury."[13] It was not all one-way traffic then. Rabbis Meir of Yavne and Jochanan would call the *evangelion* (the good news or gospel accounts of the life of Jesus) *Aven-gillayon*. It was of course a play on words but in this instance means "revelation of sin" or "falsehood of blank paper."[14] Thus in the early days blame for hostility between the two communities lay on both sides, but the church would eventually become the most powerful and therefore held the most responsibility. That responsibility became abusive. Interestingly, by the fifth century all legislation would suggest that the violence was very much one-sided.[15] Origen would go on to divide the human race into three groups, and of course he was not the last to engage in such a technique. At the bottom were pagans, which in his view included Jews; next were the average Christians; at the top was a super race of the most spiritual of Christians. It was possible for Christians to progress from the middle group through personal and spiritual development and reach the next level. Inevitably those in the bottom group had no chance; God had decreed that they should stay there. It's not difficult to see how recent history has echoed with the past. Origen would even go so far as to suggest that Plato himself was a Christian, having been influenced on a tour of Egypt four centuries before Christ by that remnant of faithful Jews who were truly Christians as opposed to the unfaithful Jews. This may sound bizarre to the modern reader but it became a popular argument at the time. In subsequent centuries all Jews were deemed to be beyond redemption, not just because they had rejected Christ but because they had persistently disobeyed God over the centuries prior to the life of Jesus. If the Christian church couldn't see the error of its own leading thinkers, then the pagans had no such difficulty in observing their lack of integrity. Summing up the message of a number of ancient pagan writers, American historian David Nirenberg (b. 1964) suggests that the pagans thought the Jews to be bad but the Christians were worse; the self-proclaimed "New Israel" couldn't even uphold the commandments God had laid down, so their claim on the covenant was illegitimate.[16]

13. Parkes, *The Conflict of the Church and the Synagogue*, 148.
14. Parkes, *The Conflict of the Church and the Synagogue*, 109.
15. Parkes, *The Conflict of the Church and the Synagogue*, 188.
16. Nirenberg, *Anti-Judaism*, 101–2.

A Hatred Defined

What is interesting is that the hostility that marked the debates within the early church were due to attempts by the so-called heretics to influence the orthodox, and not on the part of Judaism to exercise any influence.[17] Clearly the church had a problem and has continued to have problems ever since as it has wrestled with its Jewish heritage. In order to distance itself yet further from Judaism, some within the early church even began to claim that Jews knew the truth but covered it up in order to protect their own shortcomings.

In 1886, fragments of an unknown "gospel" were discovered just a few miles north of Nag Hammadi where many other manuscripts were later found. The fragments were part of an eighth- or ninth-century copy of the Gospel of Peter which was originally written in the latter part of the second century. The account bears similarities with the Synoptic Gospels, though it doesn't appear to have drawn upon Matthew or Luke. One point of departure from the canonical gospels is the reaction of those in Jerusalem to the death of Jesus on the day of the crucifixion: those that had rejected Jesus suddenly realised the error of their ways and pleaded with Pilate to put guards at the tomb.[18] Another work, the Acts of Pilate, written in the mid-second to mid-third century, records that a meeting was convened by the high priest which concluded that Jesus had indeed fulfilled the ancient prophecies but elected to keep this secret lest they be punished by the people. These accounts are of course unlikely to be historically accurate. What they actually do is reflect the teaching of the church at the time of their composition and, more importantly for us, the church's view on the Jews. The spin of the early church writers was such that contempt could only grow; in their view not only had the Jews rejected the Messiah, but they knew it and because of their stubborn pride they couldn't admit it. They were therefore destined to suffer. The screw really began to turn once the Emperor embraced Christianity in 312 and eventually made it the state religion in 325.

The manner in which Christianity became attractive to Constantine (r. 324–337) is not entirely clear. We know that he ordered the symbol of the cross to be placed on the shields of his soldiers before their battle with Maxentius at Milvian Bridge in 312, his great rival to the role of Emperor. But why did he do this? Some have claimed that he had witnessed a debate between a bishop and a rabbi where they argued, naturally, about which

---

17. Parkes, *The Conflict of the Church and the Synagogue*, 96.
18. Erhman, *Lost Scriptures*, 33.

religion had God's favor. The rabbi displayed his power by whispering the name of God into the ear of a bull and the bull promptly died. Not to be outdone, the bishop brings the bull back to life. Another claim is that Constantine saw the cross in the sky before battle and took it as an omen. A stronger possibility is that he was influenced by his recently-converted mother Helena! Whatever the reason for the embracing of the Christian faith by the soon-to-become ruler in the western half of the now-divided empire, it was a momentous event.

The acceptance of Christianity by someone of such import was one of the big turning points in history and heralded a new age. The Roman Empire had been struggling. It had been forced to adopt great changes to its structures as it faced environmental catastrophe and growing threats from its enemies on its borders. Over-intensive farming, which had led to desertification of once-fertile lands, and deforestation right across the Mediterranean resulted in food shortages and meant the Empire was weaker than it had been for a very long time. It was in the interests of the authorities to keep the peace within its borders because any instability could render the Empire even more vulnerable. This gave the Christian church the ideal opportunity to influence the state as never before.

The upper classes of Roman society embraced Christianity in what Parkes would describe as superficial form.[19] Nevertheless this did not bode well for Jews; as a consequence of costly wars they had lost any popularity they might have had previously amongst the privileged echelons.

In 339 CE, conversion to Judaism had been made illegal; anyone convicted of doing so risked losing their property. Christians were forbidden from marrying Jews and any Jew who had taken a Christian in marriage was condemned to death. Such legislation was robustly enforced because any unrest or instability within the empire that could be avoided was jumped upon.

Within thirteen years of Constantine adopting the cross as the emblem under which his soldiers should fight, Christianity was declared the state religion. This brought with it new responsibilities and new powers. The church was now in a position to undermine and eliminate any rival claim to influence with the state as the latter grew weaker by the year. Constantine was seen to have somehow fulfilled the vision of Jesus: he was all-victorious. While Jesus had been killed by his enemies, Constantine triumphed over

---

19. Parkes, *The Conflict of the Church and the Synagogue*, 157.

them.[20] A great basilica was to be built over the recently-identified location of Calvary and the tomb of Jesus; it would stand proudly overlooking the site of the ancient temple, now laid waste as testimony to the failure of the Jews to satisfy God and the failure of pagan religions.

A little over a decade after Christianity had become the state religion, the state appeared powerless against the bishops. One later example is the case of a destroyed Mesopotamian synagogue in Callanicum: it had been set ablaze on the apparent instruction of the local bishop. At the time the law forbade assaulting Jews and damaging Jewish places of worship, so the local governor, backed by Emperor Theodosius (r. 379–395), ordered the bishop to pay for rebuilding the synagogue. On hearing of the Emperor's support for the governor's actions, Ambrose (340–397), bishop of Milan, became involved, claiming that supporting Jews would endanger Theodosius's salvation. In any case, Ambrose stated, the destruction of the synagogue could not be deemed a crime as it was a house of unbelief and a place where Christ was denied. Ambrose went on to say that the priests had attempted to calm the mob but when Jews insulted them and the name of Christ, the priests could only do their duty and respond accordingly.[21] Therefore the destruction of the synagogue, in Ambrose's eyes, was the fault of the Jews. If we were ever in doubt that events over the last century are echoes of the past then here is an example: Jews suffer at the hands of others because "they bring it on themselves." There will be plenty more examples later of this insidious claim. Eventually Theodosius's support waned as he became convinced by pressure from Ambrose that his actions would strengthen the case of the Jews. However his decision was sealed when Ambrose reminded him that during the reign of the western Emperor Maximus (reigned 383–388) a synagogue in Rome had been burnt down; when Maximus sought to restore public order the Christians claimed he was a Jew. That was enough to convince Theodosius. Such was the loathing and the fear of Jews that to be called a Jew was the ultimate insult.[22]

Earlier, Emperor Julian (reigned 361–363) rejected Christianity and appeared to have some sympathy for the Jews, but it was merely a case of needs must, a form of *realpolitik*. His apparent support was in part a consequence of his neo-paganist views that held Christianity in a greater degree of mistrust than Judaism. It was Julian's view that Christianity was merely

---

20. Nirenberg, *Anti-Judaism*, 110.
21. Abel, *The Roots of Antisemitism*, 174–76.
22. Nirenberg, *Anti-Judaism*, 118.

a Galilean superstition. In his mind the church was a threat to his powers, and judging by the evidence in previous years his fears were not without justification. Another threat was just as existential and further to the east: the Persians were a force to be reckoned with and Julian's best form of defence was attack. Planning a war in the region meant that he really needed the Jews in the area to offer their support; they had already fought two great battles against Roman generals and there was no reason to doubt they wouldn't do so again. As a sop, Julian praised the Jewish patriarch Hillel II and even suggested that he might rebuild the temple at his own expense once the war was won. We shall never know if his promise would have been fulfilled because Julian died during the campaign aged just thirty-three. What we do know is that his words were void of integrity, and his true feelings were deeply negative toward the Jews, believing them to be a godforsaken race. Normal hostilities resumed on his death and within a short space of time even harsher measures against Jews were brought in under Gratian (reigned 375–383).

It was during this period that John Chrysostom (349–407) was active. Hailed as a saint by the church, much loved by church leaders down the centuries because of his asceticism and Biblical scholarship, Chrysostom was, nevertheless, a fervent opponent of Judaism. He opposed Emperor Julian's suggestion that the temple be rebuilt because he believed that a temple-less Judaism fulfilled the prophecies of Jesus; if the temple were to be revived then the teaching of Jesus would surely be undermined.[23] His opinion of Jews was such that his writings against them are difficult to stomach describing them as pitiful, miserable, obstinate, stiff-necked, murderous and always rebellious against God.[24] His definitions were to be repeated again and again down the centuries not least at Nuremburg rallies and in Munich beer kellars in the mid-twentieth century. Scholars are divided on whether his mother's beliefs influenced Chrysostom: some claim her to be a pagan, others a Christian. It may have been something in his childhood, as is so often the case that caused such contempt in the mind of young Chrysostom. He was born and grew up in Antioch, the home of a Jewish community, so even though Judaism no longer had influence in the Empire, something must have happened at some point to make Chrysostom so vehement. What we do know is that Chrysostom was baptised around the age of twenty and went on to an illustrious career within the church, eventually becoming

---

23. Nirenberg, *Anti-Judaism*, 116.
24. Nirenberg, *Anti-Judaism*, 113.

archbishop of Constantinople in 397 at the age of forty-eight. Chrysostom accused the Jews not only of ignorance but also of theft, greed and treason. His views on Jews were so convincing that other Christian leaders sought to emulate them in successive generations. These stereotypes would echo down the centuries, repeated generation after generation, and forever fixing utter contempt in the mind of many Christians, even where they would never have encountered a single Jew. When Chrysostom was informed by Christian visitors of a synagogue where holy books could be found, he simply swept their enthusiasm aside by reminding them that the holy ark had once been captured and placed in the temple of Dagon, which didn't sanctify the place. Similarly the presence of holy books could not alter the fact that the synagogue was an insult.[25] He was especially concerned that Jews could influence individual Christians, which was sufficient reason for contempt per se. It doesn't take a Freudian psychologist to wonder what had gone on in the home or streets of Chrysostom's Antioch. We can only speculate on why Chrysostom was so virulent in his hatred of Jews. This is probably of little real use, but what we can agree on is that Chrysostom's legacy was a dark one. He firmly believed that Jews should be hated for all eternity; indeed he was quite clear that they should be killed. To justify such a view he would draw upon the Parable of the Pounds: "As for these enemies of mine who did not want me to be king over them—bring them here and slaughter them in my presence."[26]

A near-contemporary of Chrysostom was that great church father Augustine (354–430). Augustine was a man of his time and also therefore a strong critic of Judaism and Jews. He likened them to Cain who had killed his brother Abel. After killing their brother Jesus they would become as abject as Cain himself. Drawing on Psalm 59, he argued that they were not to be killed but scattered across the world with no settled home as indeed they had been after the fall of Jerusalem in 135. This was so that the world would be reminded of their errors. "Do not kill them, or my people may forget, make them totter by your power and bring them down."[27]

To suggest that all relations between Jews and Christians ceased, however, would be inaccurate. Chrysostom had raged about Christians attending Passover. He argued that to share in a celebration of a festival that had once marked the betrayal of the Jews and the execution of Jesus

---

25. Abel, *The Roots of Antisemitism*, 165.
26. Luke 19:27.
27. Ps 59:11.

was anathema.[28] He ranted about women supporting the synagogue; one group had even helped fund the building of a synagogue at Apamea.[29] So it is clear that some good relations existed. Sadly we don't have video diaries of ordinary people trying to live alongside their neighbors, only the manuscripts of those who sought to drive public opinion and the theologies of the church. But we can read between the lines and from their condemnations and the legislation that was drawn up to control behavior we can conclude that the early church fathers didn't have total influence over those that preferred good relations. Take, for example, the fact that Jewish farmers were clearly admired by their Christian colleagues when the latter called on the former to bless their fields; we know this because the church became nervous about such a practice, believing it to be weakening the link between the people and God. Anyone caught seeking the blessing of Jews upon their fields would be excommunicated.[30] We also know that at the time of Constantine it became necessary to identify a different date for Easter and avoid Passover, which would indicate that the two communities had been continuing to honor the same date. Despite this there is evidence to suggest that the practice of linking Easter with Passover continued for centuries thereafter. We also know that many of the church fathers such as Justin, Clement, Origen, and Jerome, to name but a few, employed Jewish scholars to teach the traditions of Judaism and, in Jerome's case, Hebrew. Some might suggest that they did so in order to sharpen their criticism of Judaism but it may well have been that they were using such knowledge not necessarily to criticise Jews but to condemn Christian heretics.

Tragically, two events early in the fifth century would find echoes across Europe time and again in later centuries, right down to recent times. In 414 Jews were expelled from the city of Alexandria, a place where they had lived for centuries; in fact it was the longest established community in the diaspora. It all began over an argument in a theater. It is often true to say that some of the most vicious of conflicts begin over something that appeared insignificant at the outset. But some events have a habit of getting out of hand; and on this occasion get out of hand it did. It was claimed that a disturbance caused by a disciple of Bishop Cyril occurred during a theatrical performance and some Jews accosted him and handed him over to the authorities. The local prefect was not on good terms with the bishop and the

28. Abel, *The Roots of Antisemitism*, 166.
29. Abel, *The Roots of Antisemitism*, 165.
30. Abel, *The Roots of Antisemitism*, 170.

disciple was tortured and killed. On being threatened by the bishop, who had possibly believed that the prefect was under Jewish influence, the Jews attacked the local Christians. Following the Sunday service the counter attack began and the Jews were expelled.[31] A year later in 415, the church historian Socrates recorded that Jews in Inmestar, Syria had conducted a ritual murder during the festival of Purim. Purim celebrates the survival of Jews against all the odds when Haman, the Persian, as recorded in the book of Esther, was planning to massacre them in the fifth-century BCE. It had been customary for the celebrants to hang an effigy of Haman on a gallows. It was reported in 415 that a group of drunken Jews (for Purim is a time to celebrate) kidnapped a Christian boy and hanged him on a cross instead. There followed a pogrom.[32] It was not to be the last occasion when Jews would be accused of kidnapping a Christian child for a ritual murder as we shall read later. Variants have been promoted over the centuries with an upsurge in the myth of the so-called "blood libel" in the medieval period. Even in the present century, Israeli personnel engaged in rescue work in earthquake-stricken Haiti in 2010 were accused of harvesting the organs of victims for shipment back home. Similar claims have been made of Israeli forces on the bodies of terrorists, kept alive until their organs could be removed for the purpose of Jewish patients. The events of today are certainly echoes of past events.

A decade after the Alexandrian pogrom and the Syrian blood libel of 415, an event became a punctuation in the history of the relationship thus far even though it was outside the influence of Christian persecution. The spiritual leader of Judaism Gamaliel VI died without issue. After three and a half centuries of leadership the House of Hillel had come to an end; so too the office of Jewish patriarch when it was officially closed by the Emperor of the day, Theodosius II (r. 408–450). Gamaliel had seen his influence slip further and further during his time as patriarch. Edicts forbid him to adjudicate in disputes between Christians and Jews and legislation was introduced that meant Jews were no longer permitted to own Christian slaves. With his death, the center of Jewish influence shifted even further from Jerusalem as it relocated to Babylonia. This left Jews across the west even more isolated and vulnerable than they had ever been. Exposed to the growing power of the Christian church, that vulnerability would be a key factor in the coming centuries.

31. Abel, *The Roots of Antisemitism*, 178.
32. Abel, *The Roots of Antisemitism*, 179.

Chapter 3

Darkening Times

THE EARLY MIDDLE AGES or the early medieval period of European history, the fifth to tenth century, are not known as the Dark Ages for nothing. It is not that they were darker in terms of the barbarity of the period compared to other centuries but that we have less information to go on; the source material is not as prevalent as the periods that preceded or followed these centuries. However there is more than enough information available for us to draw some conclusions about the relationship between Jews and their neighbors.

The centuries following the embracing of Christianity by the Roman Empire and the subsequent collapse of that empire featured dramatic fluctuations in the fortunes of the Jewish communities. As we have already seen, the period began with a degree of persecution as restrictions and prohibitions on Jewish communities at the hands of their rulers took hold. More often than not these were based on somewhat dubious theological views devised to explain away some of the difficulties the church was having with its understanding as to why the Messiah was rejected and killed.

By the end of the period the situation began to show signs of an even deeper crisis in the relationship between the communities. As the following eleventh century played out, the greatest explosion of hatred on the part of those professing to be Christian occurred at massive cost to the Jewish communities of Europe. The Crusade of 1096 was a turning point in the relationship as hordes of baptised Christians swept across the continent enroute to the Holy Land, purporting to liberate it but choosing to massacre Jews, the "infidel in (their) midst," along the way. As the influence of the

Darkening Times

church grew, so too did the anti-Judaism that would frequently spill over into bloodshed and set the tone for centuries to come.

More often than not, the fortunes of Jews across Europe during the fifth to tenth centuries depended very much upon factors well outside their control. Their welfare was usually determined by events going on all around them, events to which Jews were little other than bystanders; Jews could have done little or nothing to prevent the implementation of persecution and the outpouring of hatred. What had seemed to be a world in which they were at worst tolerated with suspicion turned into a world of fear and darkness as forced conversion or death awaited them. As we shall see, even at the most violent of times Jews could not bring themselves round to believing that their neighbors would offer anything but support and protection. Like their descendants a millennium later they were wrong to make such assumptions; even those whom they had trusted often turned their backs on their predicament or even joined in with the theft of property and mass killing.

But all that tended to be towards the end of the period we are currently focusing on in this chapter; up until then the difficulties Jews tended to face were short-lived in historical terms and less challenging than later times. One of the reasons for this was because the Christian church or others whom the Jews found themselves under control had their hands full with greater threats to their power, authority, and influence. Generally speaking, it was only when Jews had a growing influence over their neighbors that some form of hostility was brought upon them. Infighting within the Christian church tended to be the prime reason why Jewish communities were able to go about their lives without much interference. Combatting heresies within the church was a time-consuming exercise, so it left little energy for challenging others. Therefore the Jews would benefit from the battle being waged elsewhere.

One Jewish community in Europe probably fared better than most during this period, indeed almost as well as the flourishing Babylonian community to the east: the one that had existed in Spain since nigh on the dispersion of Jews following the destruction of the temple and the fall of Jerusalem in 70 and 135 CE respectively. Despite the fact that their influence over the rest of the population in Spain was significant, unlike their counterparts elsewhere they did not face the hostility brought on by envy and fear. Bernard Lazare would claim that there were times when Spain could easily have become a Jewish country[1], such was the influence of the community in all walks of life. The church would not succeed in removing the Jews until 1492 and even then only after a long and determined struggle.

After the Visigoths conquered Spain in the fifth century CE, the Jews continued to enjoy relative freedom. This was because their new rulers were more concerned with oppressing Catholics, who were seen as a greater threat to their rule than anyone else. Then in 591, the King was converted to Catholicism and along with it came the almost inevitable persecution of Jews. Again a warped theological viewpoint, blaming Jews for their rejection of Jesus and their alleged complicity in his death, brought the unjustified "retribution." The restrictions that had been imposed earlier on Jews elsewhere in the world were swiftly brought into being: the prohibition of circumcision and dietary laws, the ability to testify against Christians, and holding any form of public office. These restrictions were held in place for a little over a century when, after the death of King Visigoth Ruderic at the Battle of Guadalete in 711, they were lifted.

For much of the remaining Dark Ages, many Jews stayed upbeat with increasing confidence, prosperity, and influence, and were not especially discriminated against. As noted earlier, church leaders were likely to focus their hostility on their coreligionists whom they deemed a threat or judged as engaging in heresy, which tended to mean that Jewish communities could go about their business free of much hassle. This allowed many Jews to become renowned and valued by their neighbors. Some became known as great linguists. Their skill in this field was probably as a consequence of the fact that many were engaged in trade across many regions. Some became great landowners and effective farmers. In most places they were even given the freedom to live by their own laws.[2]

The language of most Jews across Europe at the time was French because for many of them their most recent ancestry had been in France. As a consequence of effective trading and the open borders Jews were confident enough to move out into a wider area, even reaching as far as Prague.[3] On occasion Jews would be granted privileges such as being exempt from road tolls[4] which greatly increased their ability to engage in trade. The eleventh-century bishop of Speyer, Rudiger Huzmann, claimed that granting

---

1. Lazare, *Antisemitism: Its History and Causes*, 52.
2. Poliakov, *The History of Antisemitism: Volume 1*, 29.
3. Poliakov, *The History of Antisemitism: Volume 1*, 35.
4. Stow, *Alienated Minority*, 98.

privileges to Jews, including a cemetery and kosher slaughterhouses, were pragmatic means to enhance the city. Many Jews fleeing pogroms in Mainz and Worms took refuge there.[5] So it would be true to claim that much of the freedom that Jews may have experienced during this period was not as a result of Christian charity but either good fortune in that their rulers were engaged in other disputes and conflicts, or because of the fact that they were merely a means to an end: the improvement of a city and increasing its wealth.

Nevertheless Jews seized the opportunities that the circumstances in this period offered them. As well as economic improvement, newfound freedom allowed for an upsurge in scholarly pursuits. Along the Seine and Rhine many became famous for their writings and remained influential for centuries to come.

It was only as Jews began to rattle the cages of the powerful or to be seen as an economic threat to their non-Jewish neighbors that envy and recriminations arose. When their influence upon Christians began to grow, some church leaders began to eye them suspiciously. Fearful of losing members of their flock to a Judaism that offered much, a reaction was inevitable. Probably the most documented hostility of the period in France came from Archbishop Agobard of Lyons (779–840). Agobard was reckoned by many to be one of the most enlightened people of his generation but this did not prevent him from becoming obsessed with the Jewish community. Following a dispute with the Emperor over the impact of Judaism on the Christian community, in which Agobard called for restrictions to be put on the Jews, the archbishop was banished into exile. Even this did not stop him from writing hostile polemics against the Jews. Some scholars argue that Agobard was sowing a seed that would eventually become the medieval anti-Judaism that did so much damage to the Jewish communities across Europe. Agobard's attacks were always based on theological grounds and as the influence of the church grew, even relatively secular rulers could not ignore his hostility.

It was over the next two centuries that the relative peace and freedom for Jews would become increasingly tenuous. But even the sporadic outburst of violence and the occasional imposition of restraints were nothing compared to what lay ahead. This fluctuation in fortunes was to come to an abrupt and violent end when rumors began emanating from Jerusalem. This is another occasion when the present rhymes with the past. It was in

---

5. Stow, *Alienated Minority*, 99.

1095 that rumors spread across Europe that the holy sites in Jerusalem were being desecrated. It didn't take long for indignation to grow into furor and the furor into massacres.

Islam had arrived in the Holy Land as early as 636, just four years after the death of Muhammad, and Jerusalem fell in 638. In 691/692 the Dome of the Rock replaced an earlier Islamic structure built over the summit of Mount Moriah, the site of the temple's holy of holies, where it is said that Abraham was to have sacrificed Isaac, and the place where it is claimed that Muhammad ascended into heaven. For a few decades after its construction Jews continued to return to the Holy City from what is modern-day Iran and Iraq. They were eventually banned from praying on the site of the former temple in 720; that ban remained in force throughout Islamic rule and continues to this day. In the early ninth century, relations between Charlemagne (742–814), the king of the Franks, and the ruler of Jerusalem Caliph Haroun al-Sharid (766–809) were good, partly because the Caliph wanted to divide the Christian empires to his west. Charlemagne was permitted to become the custodian of the Christian holy sites and even construct a Christian quarter around the Holy Sepulcher. The Holy Sepulcher was a basilica originally built by Helen the mother of Constantine in the fourth century over what is traditionally believed to be Calvary and Christ's empty tomb. The Turks eventually replaced the Arabs in the Islamic Empire and Jerusalem was on occasion a battleground once again. However, the Holy Sepulcher survived, not least thanks to the provision of bribes to the rulers. But in 935 part of the Holy Sepulcher was converted into a mosque, and three years later on Palm Sunday, Christians were attacked. A generation later greater payments were demanded of the Christian community as a guarantee for their safety. Eventually the Holy Sepulcher was badly damaged by fire and the patriarch burnt at the stake. There followed a turbulent century and the fortunes of both Jews and Christians in the city fluctuated. In 1073 a central Asian army captured the city and massacred three thousand Muslims, including those that had sought refuge in the mosques. After a brief period of relative tolerance things took a turn for the worse with pilgrims being slaughtered by Jerusalem's new rulers. The Crusades were about to be unleashed.[6]

It took time for the news to reach the west but once it did, legitimate concerns turned to unwarranted violence against those who had no say in the events in the Holy Land. It was claimed that the Jews had been

---

6. Montefiore, *Jerusalem: the Biography*.

Darkening Times

responsible for encouraging the Muslim authorities to destroy the Holy Sepulcher. It became acceptable to many that Jews anywhere should bear the responsibility; this was despite the fact that Jews in the Holy Land were being as badly treated by their Islamic rulers as the Christians were. In Europe Jews faced either forced conversion, expulsion, or death. The ferocity of the onslaught was close to unprecedented. Having experienced a fairly tolerant period where they had enjoyed good relations with their Christian neighbors, and mixed more freely than they had done for some time, the Jews became easy targets. In a terrible kind of prequel to events of almost a thousand years later, Jews refused to believe the rumors that were reaching them about hordes attacking Jewish communities elsewhere. They simply could not accept that this would happen to them: they had been settled for some time; they were on good terms with their neighbors; no harm could possibly come to them. Just as their descendants in Nazi-occupied lands were to discover in the 1940s, they were tragically wrong. For example, on hearing of attacks elsewhere many in the Jewish community in Worms chose to take refuge in the bishop's palace while some stayed in their homes, completely dismissing the possibility that they were to meet the same fate as nearby communities. Once those that had remained in their homes were killed, the attackers moved on to the palace. The bishop offered the sheltering Jews conversion as a means of avoiding attack; when they declined he had them killed anyway.[7] This seems to have been a common feature at this time: the Jews in much of Europe preferred, though not exclusively so, to opt for death rather than convert. Only in Spain does there appear to have been a significant number of Jews that chose to convert.[8]

It became a common practice to blackmail the Jews into handing over their wealth as a form of protection, only for them to be murdered afterwards. Again our recent past was not without precedent. Some of the violence had little or nothing to do with the events in the Holy Land and more to do with opportunism, something that would feature again and again in the course of history. Jewish homes and businesses were looted, individuals attacked and robbed. The excuse given was that Jews had somehow been complicit in the destruction of the Holy Sepulcher and that therefore it was legitimate to attack Jews everywhere. The truth is that many mobs were nothing other than violent thugs bent on making something out of the situation.

---

7. Poliakov, *The History of Antisemitism: Volume 1*, 43.
8. Poliakov, *The History of Antisemitism: Volume 1*, 45.

Numerous church leaders thought it curious to fight the infidel in the east when so many of "the guilty" were on their doorstep. Indeed, thanks to the warped theology that Jews were responsible for the rejection of Jesus and his death, not to mention their continuing reluctance to accept the teaching of the Church, it was argued that the Jews were guiltier than the Muslims. However, as in every persecution there are those who swim against the current and it is important to note that not all church leaders felt the same. Not only did these leaders see the attacks as unjustifiable even if they believed there was a legitimate concern about the holy sites, but they recognised the unruly nature of the mobs conducting their violent attacks. A number of bishops sought to prevent massacres by urging the organized Crusaders to show some restraint. Bernard of Clairvaux (1090–1153) was concerned that by wiping out the Jews there would be none left to convert, thus denying the church's mission. This was surely a back-handed way of showing support if there ever was one.[9] Right up until our recent past it was not unusual for church leaders to argue that the presence of a downtrodden, persecuted Jewry was necessary to highlight the judgment of God for the alleged complicity in the death of Jesus and their continuing rejection of him. Indeed over the course of recent decades the formation of the state of Israel has been, as we shall see later, a challenge for those whose theology cannot cope with the fortunes of Israel being restored.

Once the Crusaders left an area and moved on, many surviving Jews sought to rebuild relations with their neighbors. Although the king of the Germans, Emperor Henry IV (1050–1106), authorized those Jews that had been forcibly converted to return to their own religious practices[10] he had shown great ambivalence toward them.[11] Pope Clement III (1029–1100) opposed such a move and instigated an edict stating that once a Jew had converted he or she could not rescind it. The edict was to remain in place a millennium later.

There were other developments around this period that, when compared with the Crusades, seemed less significant at the time. Nevertheless they would have a lasting impact and their mutations would help foster hatred over the centuries down to the present day. The first of these developments was dramatic presentation of the gospel, especially the passion story.

---

9. Poliakov, *The History of Antisemitism: Volume 1*, 49.
10. Poliakov, *The History of Antisemitism: Volume 1*, 46.
11. Stow, *Alienated Minority*, 97.

Darkening Times

The Good Friday liturgy of the Catholic Church had been amended in the ninth century to identify the Jews as a race apart. Up until then they had been included in the prayers as a group, alongside pagans and others, which could find salvation, but the changes indicated that there was no such opportunity to be given to the "fallen race." This view couldn't do anything other than play a thoroughly detrimental role in fostering further the alleged complicity of Jews in the death of Jesus whenever the Good Friday narrative was presented. It was certainly an effective way of whipping up the crowd.

Dramatic presentations of the gospel in this period were an innovation; up until then church services tended to be somber occasions with little or no drama. Anxious to not emulate Judaism in any way, churches had sought to avoid being as colorful as the synagogues and therefore ended up rather austere with the liturgies being somewhat turgid. But all this was about to change.

When dramatic presentation as a means of communicating Christ's passion grew in popularity, greater numbers of participants were needed, so it became necessary for the laity to take part, broadening further the possibility of fostering hatred. Increasingly cities sought to outdo each other in their quest for greater elaboration. The developments were rapid and due to their immense popularity performances spilt out of the church building into the public square, drawing in ever increasing numbers. With these great festivals frenzy amongst the crowds was nurtured. Over the years it would become a feature of Good Friday services to end with worshippers wanting to vent their anger at the betrayal and death of Christ, and if there were Jews in the community, then they were the obvious target. This was not something that would easily fade away in the following years, far from it: the tragedy was that it would persist and grow. Right across Europe, well into the last century, Jews would justifiably fear Good Friday; they would shut up shop, board up their windows, bar their doors and stay at home. It is ironic that John's account of the gospel claimed that on the night of the resurrection disciples of Jesus would hide behind locked doors "for fear of the Jews"[12] (a verse we have already considered) when actually over the centuries it has been Jews who have had to hide themselves behind locked doors for fear of the Christians. The seeds of anti-Judaism had been sown in the later gospel accounts and the writings of the church fathers. It had been present on different levels at various intervals over the centuries

---

12. John 20:19.

and had erupted into despicable acts of violence during the Crusades. It now found expression in a way that would ensure its longevity through the Good Friday liturgy and presentation. As a consequence of using the term *pro perfidis Judaeis* in the Good Friday liturgy (meaning unfaithful Jews), the phrase "perfidious Jews" stuck which came to be defined as duplicitous, treacherous, and dishonest. It was not until 1958 that Pope John XXIII (1881–1963) insisted that the term be omitted. When on Good Friday 1963 a deacon used the old liturgy and included it, the pope insisted that the prayer be repeated but without the term. It wasn't until the 1970s that the Anglican communion revised their Good Friday collect to avoid such contempt of the Jewish community.

Along with the dramatic presentation of the passion narrative came more illustrative forms of communication in the form of paintings, murals, carvings and eventually stained glass. These became media by which the growing number of anti-Jewish myths could be conveyed. We begin to see traces of what would become known as *synagoga and ecclesia*, the former represented by a woman, head hung in shame, complete with broken staff, Hebrew Scriptures falling from her hand, ankles sometimes in chains, and always blindfolded to highlight her spiritual blindness. While *ecclesia* was an upright bride adorned by a crown, holding a strong staff and either a chalice or a model of a church or cathedral. This and other symbolism that came to be developed in the medieval period will be considered in our next chapter. But there is one more development in the eleventh century that warrants introduction now. Like the Good Friday liturgy and the comparison of *synagoga* with *ecclesia*, it had a lasting impact upon the image of Jews that their detractors would seek to present in the coming centuries.

It is documented that around 1084 the inhabitants of Worms paraded the dead body of a Christian around the city claiming that the Jews had exhumed it, kept it in boiling water and then used the water to poison the wells.[13] This was not dissimilar to the Syrian blood libel of 415, and there may well have been other occasions in the intervening years. As we shall see in the next chapter, variations of this allegation would be propagated across the world over the next centuries and the abuse of dead bodies remains an anti-Semitic trope to this day. Known as the "blood libel," the "victims" would become martyrs of the church and their tombs the destination for Christian pilgrims.

---

13. Stow, *Alienated Minority*, 109.

As this chapter draws to a close I think it is important to underline the case that as the church grew in influence so too did its hostility toward Jews. In the medieval period even fairly non-religious rulers would be fearful of the power the church. As a consequence they would often rather persecute Jews than upset the bishop. In the first of his four-volume work on *antisemitism* Poliakov writes:

> "Each time medieval Europe was swept by a great movement of faith, each time the Christians set out to face the unknown in the name of the love of God, hatred of the Jews was fanned into flame virtually everywhere. And the more the pious impulses of the heart sought satisfaction in action, the worse the Jews' lot became."[14]

---

14. Poliakov, *The History of Antisemitism: Volume 1*, 49.

Chapter 4

Stigmatization and Segregation

If the Dark Ages were volatile for the Jews, the following centuries would prove even more so; with an ever-deepening hostility and increasing frequency of attacks, the fate of the Jews was precarious to say the least. The attacks of 1096 were more than just an immediate and apparently convenient response to the hatred fostered by the loss of the Holy City, they were becoming a means by which society could be "purified." Today we would identify such action as a form of social, ethnic, or religious cleansing. As the centuries progressed further assaults became ever more likely with the church seeking to achieve an even firmer grip on power and influence.

Later Crusades would result in renewed attacks, not always as a consequence of heightened emotions over the need to recapture the Holy Land or to purge Europe of non-Christians, but rather as a consequence of pure and simple greed. After all, attacks during intervening periods could not be blamed on an infidel occupying Jerusalem. It is ironic that during this time Jews would be cast as money-oriented when so many had been forced into usury, a profession that was deemed by the church as unsuitable for Christians but wholly acceptable for Jews. It is equally ironic that when this resulted in temporary wealth for some members of the Jewish community they should be envied, robbed, bankrupted, and even killed at whim for engaging in a business that they had little or no choice over. The term "used and abused" springs to mind. This trope would follow Jews down the centuries right up until the present day.

This chapter will consider the ferocity of the attacks on Jews and the often spurious reasons given for such attacks, not least the additional irony

Stigmatization and Segregation

that Jewish communities having been ghettoized, Jews were then accused of being elitist and separatist.

Anti-Judaism was well-established by the second millennium; almost a thousand years of polemical sermons and writings had ensured that Christian hatred of Jews was seen to be justified on theological grounds and the claim to be "doing God's will." However, the Christian church was also building on a sociological hatred that had been in existence even long before the birth of Jesus. This long-standing hatred continued in those places where Jews butted up against communities other than Christian, i.e. the Islamic world. The myths about Jews that sprang up in the church of the Middle Ages were often based on the suspicion and fear that had their origins in ancient Greece, Rome, and Egypt.[1] Greeks, of course, placed great value on debate and social interaction, but the fact that Jews believed it necessary to refrain from certain foods and to avoid being contaminated by certain practices, not least the worship of pagan gods, ensured their stigmatization. It is a common response to become suspicious of those who keep themselves to themselves or to even consider that they think more highly of themselves than they actually do. Much of the hostile sermon-writing of the medieval period featured the suspicion and fear engendered by the apparent separateness of Jews.[2] It is often conveniently overlooked that it was necessary for Jews to gather in their own communities within a town or city, for they needed to maintain a *minyan*, a quorum for worship. Therefore it was not unusual to find whole streets that were inhabited by Jews, thus ensuring that the dietary laws could be upheld with their own slaughterhouse, that *mikvehot*, (ritual baths) could be provided and so on; all the things that were required for Jews to uphold their faith meant that it was preferable to congregate together. This only fueled the suspicions that the "Jews were up to no good," that the "Jews thought of themselves as above everyone else," etc. It would have been impossible for Jews to maintain their faith in rural isolation; the immediacy of coreligionists was a must for the survival of their faith. Clearly non-Jews, and indeed the Church, were not confident enough in themselves to do anything other than allow such suspicion to grow into an ever-deepening hatred. When things went wrong for the wider community, even the inexplicable, one explanation could always be that the Jews had something to do with it.

---

1. Gregg, *Young Devils, Women and Jews*, 175.
2. Gregg, *Young Devils, Women and Jews*, 182.

Even when the king of Castile, Alfonso (1158–1214) fell in love with a member of the Jewish community it was argued that she had put a spell on him and the kingdom went to wrack and ruin. There was nothing left to do but have her killed and the king "rescued" from his plight. The story ends with an angel appearing to the king reminding him of his sin. The likelihood is that the woman never existed: it only came to be told 180 years after the king's death and may have been an excuse for the ruinous state of the kingdom at that time.[3]

It became a common theme in the period to look for someone to blame for the plight of a town, city or kingdom, and Jews were more often than not the easy target, from economic distress to black death, from the random murder of a child to famine; Jews and their "wicked and secretive ways" were surely responsible for any ill that fell upon the wider community.

One of the most lasting myths came to be known as the "blood libel," the alleged ritual killing by Jews of a Christian child so that his blood could be mixed in with the Passover bread. Its origins can be dated to at least the twelfth century, though we have already seen earlier that a variation of it may have been in existence long before; however, the only hard evidence we have of a more developed libel is that it was in existence from the twelfth century.

It may be shocking to discover that the first recorded act of a blood libel in this form took place in England in 1144. Jews had only arrived in England less than a century before, after the conquest by William of Normandy in 1066. In the following decades a number made their way from northern France to be part of the transformation into a system that resembled elsewhere in Europe. Because of their expertise developed on the continent, Jews were in a very good position to seize opportunities in a country that had few rivals in the world of finance. It therefore didn't take long for Jews to be viewed with suspicion and hatred. Some of the stories that had fueled attacks across Europe as a consequence of the Crusades found willing ears in the newly defeated and subdued cities of England.

In 1144, on the day before Easter, the body of a young boy named William was discovered just outside the city of Norwich. It wasn't long before the Jewish community of Norwich got the blame. It was alleged that William had been put to death by the Jews as a sacrificial act for their Passover feast. Allegations of ritual murder carried out by religious minorities was nothing new: during the Roman period early Christians were the accused

3. Nirenberg, *Anti-Judaism*, 184–85.

Stigmatization and Segregation

and there are even much later records of Jesuit missionaries to China being similarly accused.[4] But in the atmosphere of the twelfth century, in the wake of fairly recent events in England and abroad, the scene was set for a rapid growth in accusation and retribution. Some historians claim that as many as 150 blood libels were levelled against the Jews over a period of three hundred years, some without so much as a body. But in the case of William, there was a body and before long the story developed into a highly sophisticated claim that his blood had been drawn to help in the manufacture of unleavened bread. This is absolute nonsense in that Jews are strictly forbidden to consume blood in any form, but that didn't stop the people of England from engaging in a vile and deeply hostile campaign. Despite the attempt of successive popes to quell the claims and monarchs issuing edicts condemning the blatantly ridiculous claims, the blood libel took hold with the bones of the alleged victims becoming venerated in cathedrals. The body of one such victim, Little Hugh, whom we shall consider shortly, is still entombed in Lincoln Cathedral. There was money to be made out of pilgrims. Fueling hatred of Jews complete with the relics of one of their alleged victims in a secretive, mysterious, conspiratorial pact conducted by the "Christ-killer Jews" became big business. The child victim being innocent and pure became closely associated with the Christ himself. Indeed the suffering and death of William of Norwich as depicted on the fifteenth-century rood screen in Loddon, Norfolk, associates the events with the passion of Christ.[5] So closely linked to the crucifixion of Jesus is the depiction that even a regular visitor to the church could easily be forgiven for thinking that it is nothing other than a scene from the crucifixion of Christ. In the imagery even the genitals are mutilated as if the boy was violated by circumcision prior to his death.

27 years after the death of William of Norwich, virtually the entire Jewish community of Blois was wiped out by an angry mob after a blood libel, in this case without even so much as a body. As they died the Jews sang in unison the *Alenu*, a mournful confession. News of their deaths spread across Europe and the Jewish communities braced themselves for what they believed would be the inevitable; they were not mistaken. In quick succession other blood libel allegations were made and communities suffered one after another. It was even so that Jews would be blackmailed

---

4. Roth, *A Short History of the Jewish People*, 189.
5. Bale, *Feeling Persecuted*, 52.

by their Christian neighbors, to pay up or be accused of kidnapping a child that in reality had been sent by the family into hiding.

In addition to William of Norwich, other cases were reported across England, including one in Gloucester just 22 years later when a gathering to celebrate a circumcision led locals to claim that a boy by the name of Harold had been abducted, tortured, and his body thrown into the River Severn. Another led to the expulsion of Jews from Bury St. Edmunds in 1190, a full nine years after the death of a young boy called Robert at the alleged hands of Jews. Similar episodes were reported in Bristol and Winchester, the latter boasting of three such murders in 1192, 1225, and 1232.[6]

But the one that caught the imagination probably more than any other in subsequent centuries was that of Little Hugh in Lincoln (1255). This was probably as a consequence of being retold a century later by Chaucer in "The Prioress's Tale" and countless folk songs since; indeed it still occasionaly features in performances at recent folk festivals. So well-known did the story become and so venerated was Little Hugh that he came to be known as "Little Saint Hugh" to distinguish him from the actual Saint Hugh of Lincoln (1135–1200); the latter was indeed a saint and had sought to build good relations with members of the Jewish communities. But while Little Hugh was never canonized, his entry in numerous respected encyclopedias still refer to him as "Little Saint Hugh."

Little Hugh had been missing for almost a month when his body was discovered down a well on land owned by Jopin, a Jew who lived just a few yards away. The Chief Justice, John of Lexington, whose brother Henry was at the time the bishop of Lincoln, coerced Jopin to confess that the boy had been crucified by prominent members of the Jewish community that had gathered for a wedding in Lincoln. In so doing Jopin was promised a pardon. But a month later Henry III visited Lincoln, revoked the pardon and had Jopin tied to a horse and dragged through the city's streets. 92 Jews from the city, some who were just visiting for the wedding, were sent to the Tower of London and 18 of them executed.

The body of Little Hugh was buried in the south aisle of the cathedral next to the choir. An extravagant shrine was created and pilgrims from across the land made their way to pay their respects to this "crucified child." When the body was exhumed for examination during the eighteenth century, there were no signs whatsoever of the boy being crucified. The body was reinterred and the tomb, albeit in a less grand state, remains to this

---

6. Schama, *The Story of the Jews*, 309.

day. The cathedral continued to present the story in its traditional form through a notice next to the tomb, right up until 1959 when the Dean, the Very Reverend D.C. Dunlop, and the Chapter ordered its removal. A more appropriate and accurate notice replaced it, solemnly acknowledging trumped up stories of "ritual murders" of Christian boys by Jewish communities. In 2009 a more substantial plaque was placed adjacent to the tomb.

A somewhat odder claim about the Jews and blood came to be made following the earlier recognition in 1215 of the doctrine of transubstantiation. The doctrine claimed that the consecrated bread miraculously became the actual body of Jesus at the mass. It was alleged that Jews would steal a piece of the bread and deliberately pierce it with knives in order to exact further pain on the Christ. As evidence for this priests would point out that blood could be seen in the bread on occasions. A more scientific mind would today recognize that bread when stale and moldy can sometimes create scarlet patches and give the appearance of blood. But this was all that it would take for local Jews to be vilified and persecuted.[7]

The blood libel wasn't contained within the medieval period: versions of it can be found right down to the present day in various parts of the world. Some of the claims would be almost identical to those of the twelfth to fifteenth centuries while others would be a variation on the theme: Jews engaged in the killing of someone from outside their faith, desecrating the bodies, and using the blood for their own purposes (often ritualistic). One such occasion being in Damascus in 1840 when a Catholic monk and his servant disappeared which resulted in the leaders of the Jewish community sentenced to execution. The Jewish world rallied and a campaign was launched to save the accused.[8] 170 years later Syrian TV, shortly before the Civil War erupted as a consequence of the so-called Arab Spring, broadcast a drama on national TV depicting in all its gory detail the fictitious ritual killing of a Muslim child by Jews in ultra-orthodox costume. If much of the most violent forms of Judeophobia are now propagated in the Middle East, then post-Holocaust Europe is still not immune from blood libel claims. Just a year after the Second World War in 1946, Poles in Kielce went on the rampage, killing Jews whom they claimed had engaged in the ritual killing of a Christian child; the boy later turned up unharmed.[9] Other variations

---

7. Roth, *A Short History of the Jewish People*, 189–90.
8. Florence, *Blood Libel*.
9. Goldhagen, *The Devil that Never Dies*, 118.

will be referred to towards the end of the book when we consider political Judeophobia.

For now we return to the medieval period, when just as today, Jews could not win. If a plague broke out and they were amongst the first to catch it they were blamed for bringing it into the city; if they didn't catch it then they must have woven a spell on the Christian community whilst keeping themselves immune. Kings would accuse them of siding with conspirators while rebels would claim they were in allegiance with the ruler. Any heresy must surely have originated with the Jews; after all they could clearly be seen to be practicing a different faith and continued to uphold strange beliefs.[10]

Further stigmatization came with the enforcement of clothing and even badges that singled out Jews from the rest of the community. Badges were not new. Christians and Jews had been forced to wear them by their Muslim rulers in what is now Gaza during the eighth century and remained in force for centuries afterwards. By the twelfth century, Jews were forced to add further distinguishing marks on their person, to wear a lead badge around their necks with the word *Dhimmi* (non-Muslim) on it, and a belt around their waist. Jewish women were forced to wear one red shoe and one black shoe, and a small bell around their neck or on their shoes.[11]

To identify Jews and avoid contamination through their heresy or through sexual relations (it's not clear which was viewed as the more serious sin of the two at the time) they were to be set further apart from and by the Christian community. In a foretaste of later centuries it was ordered by Pope Innocent III in 1215 that a yellow badge, albeit a circle or oval, one finger wide and one half palm in length, had to be worn by all Jews when they were outside their home or quarter. It is sometimes claimed that the yellow circle represented a gold coin symbolizing the betrayal of Christ.[12] Married women were forced to wear two bands of blue on their veil or head-scarf. By 1274 Edward I of England forced every Jew from the age of seven to wear a yellow badge three inches wide and six inches in length. Elsewhere in Europe Jews were forced to wear a pointed hat, a *Judenhut*, which was often claimed to hide their satanic horns or even the mark of Cain.

---

10. Roth, *A Short History of the Jewish People*, 191.
11. Johnson, Paul, *A History of the Jews*, 204–5.
12. Reuther, *Faith and Fratricide*, 210.

Stigmatization and Segregation

It's not uncommon to find imagery in cathedrals and churches that feature the *Judenhut* in the retelling of anti-Jewish myths. Lincoln Cathedral not only contains the remains of Little Hugh but medieval stained glass that depict two such myths. The first is the Jew of Borges. In this story the son of a Jewish glass-blower makes friends with local Christian boys and they encourage him to enter the cathedral where he encounters a woman who invites him to partake in the mass. On his return home he informs his father, who promptly throws him into his blazing furnace. The woman mentioned earlier appears and opens the furnace to find that the boy is miraculously untouched by the flames. The woman happens to be Mary the mother of Jesus. The remainder of the story has not survived in the stained glass of Lincoln but we know from other documentation that it concludes with the community throwing the father into the furnace where he is consumed by the fire. As well as this retelling in Lincoln Cathedral, there is another story told in its stained glass: the myth of Theophilus. Theophilus is said to have made a pact with the devil through the "good offices" of a go-between Jew.[13] Lincoln also has an example of *Ecclesia* and *Synagoga*, located at the Judgment Porch, through which pilgrims would enter before being taken to the shrine of Little Hugh. They are larger-than-life scale sculptures either side of the south entrance door, to the east representing Christianity and to the west representing Judaism. They are in the form of women. The heads are damaged now but we know from other versions elsewhere in Europe, most notably Strasbourg, that the woman representing Christianity has a crown and her head is proudly held while the one representing Judaism is blindfolded to indicate spiritual darkness. Both hold a staff but the one that depicts Judaism is broken. The Torah scrolls fall from her finger tips and in the Lincoln version chains bind her feet with Moses and the tablets of stone round his neck peer from under them. In Strasbourg the woman representing Christianity holds a chalice while the Lincoln version holds a scale model of a cathedral. Notre Dame has its own version at the West End, interestingly refurbished in their full anti-Judaistic form during the nineteenth century. There will be more on Judeophobia in nineteenth-century France in a later chapter of the book.

Another story emanating from Lincoln tells us a great deal about the relations between Christians and Jews. It was said that at some point in the medieval period a canon of the minster fell in love with a Jewish woman in the city. They arranged to consummate their love for each other on the

---

13. Gregg, *Young Devils, Women and Jews*, 231 and 216.

night of Good Friday, no less. This was deemed by the young woman to be the most suitable night because other Jews would not be going about their business on such a night when they were likely to be attacked by Christians in an act of revenge for the death of Christ. When her father discovered them in bed together the next morning, he wanted to kill the priest but recognised him as the cousin of the bishop, so having reminded him of his sin and good fortune in being so closely related to the bishop, let him go. Later that night the canon was assigned to act as deacon to the bishop at Easter eve mass; as he stood at the altar the woman's father and a number of other Jews came to the minster door making a noise and wanting to lodge a complaint with the bishop. The canon was overcome with shame and offered to confess his sin and rededicate himself wholly to never sin again. The bishop intervened, wanting to know what had brought the Jews to the church on a day such as this. But as they were about to tell him they were all allegedly struck dumb. Believing that they had come to interrupt the mass, the bishop had them ejected. Following the service the canon felt that his prayer had been heard, confessed his sin to the bishop, and became a Cistercian monk. The story goes that together they converted the young woman who herself became a nun. It was not the first time, nor would it be the last, that a Jew would be solely blamed for an act that he or she was at best only partly responsible and that God, according to the myth, would silence Jews in their protest.[14]

As the thirteenth century drew to a close, time was running out for Jews in England. As well as the vile hostility being waged against the Jewish communities as a consequence of the myths, the financial situation was becoming parlous and unsustainable. Jews, being the money lenders of the day, would become the target for an unjust and brutal acquisition of wealth.

Despite the blood libel and other forms of stigmatization, the economic success of Jews in England during the twelfth century was great. This was as a result of expertise in financial dealings and the fact that they had little or no competition. But by the beginning of the thirteenth century things began to take a turn for the worse. King John's incompetence and failed wars meant that the exchequer was nearly bankrupt. Higher taxation was the option he took, especially of the Jews. So enormous was his demand that the Jews simply could not meet it. As a consequence many of the wealthiest were imprisoned, including Abraham of Bristol. Refusing to pay the 10,000 marks, Abraham had a tooth extracted each consecutive day

---

14. Gregg, *Young Devils, Women and Jews*, 220.

until the eighth when he committed suicide.[15] Some have wondered if this is not where Shakespeare might have got his idea for Shylock demanding a pound of flesh, albeit the Jew making the demand upon a non-Jew. As we have seen earlier, such an act as suicide was becoming a means by which Jews believed they could retain their dignity in the face of such violence.

As we have already noted the wealth of some Jews was accumulated through usury, the practice whereby a loan is made and interest is charged. Forbidden in scripture, Christians were able to force such a profession upon Jews without fear of damnation. Jews were also forbidden by the Talmud but by the end of the twelfth century the rabbis agreed that the community had to adapt itself to changing circumstances. They therefore held that it was indeed possible to lend for interest to non-Jews because it was only forbidden to do so with a coreligionist.[16] Because Jews were in the urban spaces, as noted above, and because they had been used to such practice in France and elsewhere, they were in a wonderful position to make best use of the situation. The only problem was that the king "owned" the debts and could call them in at any time. In other words the Jewish money lender was only a proxy bank for the king. If the king wished to bankrupt the money lender he could, and on occasions would. It was also decreed that on death the debts owed to the money-lender should be payable to the monarch. The king couldn't lose, but the Jew could and tragically did.

It is important to note that Jews were not the only ones engaged in usury but it became a stereotypical view of Jews. For example, large non-Jewish Italian families such as the Lombards were involved in much larger operations across Europe.[17] It is equally true that evidence suggests the wealth of the Jewish communities was on occasion exaggerated.[18] The period also marked a transition from usury to trade as shipping became a means by which trade could take place, especially via Italian shipping. This in turn gave rise to a new merchant class, from which Jews would be excluded.

As the century progressed, the economic situation in England worsened, and by 1272 when Edward I came to the throne he eyed the wealth of Jewish money-lenders with a good deal of envy. His prejudices had been fueled, if not formed, by his experience on Crusade. Edward had little

15. Poliakov, *The History of Antisemitism: Volume 1*, 78.
16. Poliakov, *The History of Antisemitism: Volume 1*, 75.
17. Poliakov, *The History of Antisemitism: Volume 1*, 76.
18. Poliakov, *The History of Antisemitism: Volume 1*, 77.

sympathy for the plight of the Jews and it didn't take long for him to prove it. Beginning with enforcing the badge of identity, noted above, on virtually every Jew in the land, Edward would go on to move whole communities of Jews to a smaller number of towns and to restrict their movements. In 1275 he forbade money-lending. Those that were also artisans and involved in an array of occupations were not permitted to enter the guilds, so the situation grew rapidly worse. Further stories and myths were recited about Jews and the fear and hostility among the non-Jewish population deepened. In 1278/9 a scandal broke out that would precipitate the end of a Jewish presence in England for the next three and a half centuries. Jews were accused of shaving a fraction off silver and gold coins; the shavings were then melted down into blocks. No one can say who was responsible; maybe some Jews and maybe some non-Jews; it mattered not, the Jews got the blame. It was known as the "coin-clipping scandal" and the Jews paid a hefty price. They were all gathered together from around the country and incarcerated in London jails. 269 Jews were hanged and in 1290 the remainder were expelled. The excuse given was that they had committed crimes and their expulsion would be in honor of Jesus Christ. The outcome was that the interest owed on the debts was not paid and the now-vacated houses of Jews became available at knock-down prices. There are many examples of profiteering from their plight with ships' captains charging extortionate prices to transport them to the continent, and in one case abandoning them on a sand bank after having extracted their fees and worldly goods.[19]

Other expulsions would occur elsewhere in Europe over subsequent centuries, most notably in Spain in 1492, but England was the first to so methodically and comprehensively implement a strategy whereby Jews were systematically targeted, rounded up, and expelled. However, events shortly after the Spanish expulsion of 1492 would lay the theological foundations for church impotence in the Holocaust of the twentieth century.

Just 25 years after the Jews were expelled from Spain, Martin Luther would begin his assault on the Catholic Church and what became known as the Reformation would get underway. Publishing his *Ninety-Five Theses* in 1517, Luther criticized the church for selling indulgences to help pay for the rebuilding of St. Peter's Basilica in Rome. Three years later he refused to retract his writings.

Luther's subsequent work would come to have a severe impact on the security of Jews throughout Europe over the centuries. Yet at the beginning,

---

19. Schama, *The Story of the Jews*, 325.

Luther harbored great hopes that his belief in justification by faith would be understood and accepted by Jews. He thought that they would readily embrace Christ as the Messiah. It was only when they didn't that he was to formulate views that are utterly abhorrent to the post-Auschwitz reader. But even more than the violent instructions in dealing with Jews, their books, and their synagogues, Luther's two kingdom doctrine was to play a very large part in the inability of the reformed churches to meet their greatest challenge during the Third Reich.

The two kingdoms doctrine held that there were two realms: the first an earthly one with God exercising rule through granting even secular powers the authority to govern; the second a heavenly realm, in which Christians by grace operate. A verse from Paul's letter to the Romans became a key text in understanding and accepting the rule of earthly authorities: "Let every person be subject to the governing authorities; for there is no authority except from God, and those authorities that exist have been instituted by God."[20] It isn't difficult to see how this understanding would make it hard for Lutherans to oppose even a secular government. Even the Calvinists, the reformed church that was well-represented along the Rhine, came to uphold the view. So Protestant Germany in the 1930s would struggle with a huge dilemma: accept that the Nazis were part of God's plan or challenge a long-established doctrine.

As we have noted, Luther had high hopes of Jewish interest and possible conversion to Christ, and his 1523 pamphlet "Jesus Christ was Born a Jew" sought to prove that Jesus was the Jewish Messiah; it was issued on numerous occasions over subsequent centuries. But 19 years later he was to publish a work that would contain 200 pages of the vilest diatribe against Jews that had been produced to date and rarely, if ever, surpassed since. Once the content becomes known to us it will come as no surprise that the Nazis would make popular editions available to the people. The uncritical mind within 1930s Germany would not take into account Luther's growing mental instability, but would merely accept it as the work of a great man. What few would realize is that Luther was by now bitter and twisted, finding it difficult to tell what was of God and what was of the devil. But the damage was done. His writing would impact not only the German people of the Nazi period but also many German cities and towns

---

20. Romans 13:1.

in his own time. Having given up on the possibility of Jews converting to Christianity, he came to believe that it was impossible for them to do so until the apocalypse.[21]

None of this is too great a surprise when the writings of Luther, even in the period of what might be seen as a more slightly more affable approach to Jews, are fully understood. The development into an openly-hostile view is plain to see. In his very first lectures at Wittenberg beginning in 1513, the young Luther took a different line to Augustine on Scripture, not least in the Psalms. While Augustine viewed the Hebrew Scriptures as being about Judaism and the Hebrews, Luther held that they were all about Christ. Therefore any failing of the people which Augustine would have seen as a failing of all humankind, Luther would argue was the inherent spiritual blindness of Jews, a blindness that was permanent until they embraced Christ as the Messiah, which, as we noted earlier, he came to believe they could not do until the apocalypse.[22]

Luther proposed that Jewish books should be confiscated, synagogues be burnt to the ground, Jews be forbidden to pray, and they be put to work or be expelled.[23] If ever there was a medieval blueprint for the Holocaust then this is it. Luther would become even more detailed and hysterical, claiming that the only explanation for their deceitful and satanic practices was that the Jews had sent their servants to gather up the "piss" and "offal" of Judas after he had hanged himself that they might drink and eat from their plates of silver and pots of gold.[24] In a precursor of how later Judeophobes would later justify their own prejudice, Luther would claim that he was merely seeking to edify the church; he had nothing personal against the Jews, you see! What he left the reader in no doubt of was his sheer hatred of Jews. On one occasion[25] he suggested that if a Jew were willing to be baptized he would take him to the Elbe Bridge, tie a stone round his neck, and push him off, "baptizing him in the name of Abraham."[26] Even in his final sermon he could not resist attacking the Jews.

---

21. Nirenberg, *Anti-Judaism*, 266.
22. Nirenberg, *Anti-Judaism*, 252–55.
23. Poliakov, *The History of Antisemitism: Volume 1*, 218.
24. Poliakov, *The History of Antisemitism:: Volume 1*, 219.
25. Poliakov, *The History of Antisemitism: Volume 1*, 223.
26. Just a few years later Ivan the Terrible did exactly that in Moscow with the entire Jewish community. Nirenberg, *Anti-Judaism*, 266.

Stigmatization and Segregation

Thankfully many princes and rulers of the sixteenth century were not swayed by Luther's rhetoric. It had been Luther's hope that Jews would be expelled en-masse and he sought to persuade the authorities to do so. But he was only partly successful and rulers actively encouraged Jews to resettle in German cities.[27] Nevertheless, his teachings could be argued to have been directly responsible for violence and expulsions in Saxony in 1537, towns in Thuringia in 1540, Brunswick in 1543 and 1553, Berlin in 1572, and Brandenburg in 1573.[28]

Four centuries later, his works were to become the staple diet for Nazified Christians in twentieth-century Germany. The 450th anniversary of Luther's birth fell just weeks after Hitler came to power in 1933. The coincidence was not an opportunity to be missed by the Nazi propaganda machine. Huge celebrations were held and the newly-installed power embraced the popular mood by adopting Luther as one of their own. At one celebration in Köningsberg, the capital of East Prussia, the local bishop and local *Gauleiter*[29] stood together as it was proclaimed that Hitler's rise to power was of divine providence.[30] In order to stem Catholic suspicion of Luther it had been claimed that Luther was merely an unwitting accomplice of Jewish action against the church, and that the schism forged by the Reformation was the fault of the Jews.[31] It wasn't the first time nor would it be the last that Jews, as victims, would be seen as the reason for their own fate; we shall return to this theme in a later chapter.

Before leaving this period and moving on to the false dawn of the Enlightenment, it is important to reference the impact disease, not least plague and in particular the Black Death, would have on the Jewish communities of Europe. As we have already noted Jews were damned if they went down with illness on the grounds that they must have brought it into the community, and damned if they didn't in the mistaken belief that they must have been engaged in some form of magical ritual that would render them immune. The Black Death decimated the population of Europe and the Mediterranean region and brought society to its knees; figures vary but it is often claimed that the death toll was at least 70 million and could well have been around 200 million: around 30–60 percent of the population. It

---

27. Stow, *Alienated Minority: the Jews of Medieval Europe*, 300.
28. Nirenberg, *Anti-Judaism*, 262.
29. Local leader of the Nazi Party.
30. Steigman-Gall, *The Holy Reich*, 1.
31. Steigman-Gall, *The Holy Reich*, 53.

probably began in central Asia around 1343 and within just a few years had spread across Europe via the trade routes, which is one reason why Jews were held responsible: they were after all the great travelers and traders of their day. As the populace began to wonder where the disease had come from they considered it to be of cosmic significance, and who else could be in cahoots with the devil other than the Jews? Some protagonists even formed bands known as "flagellants" who sought to avert the divine wrath that had allowed such a pestilence and obtain remission of sins by travelling from city to city across Germany and into France singing hymns, whipping up the crowd, and almost inevitably ending in the mass murder of Jews.[32]

But there can be no justification for the onslaught Jewish communities would face at the hands of their Christian oppressors. There is nothing new about modern-day conspiracy theories; we now know that the plague was spread by rat fleas on board trading vessels.

With each wave of the Black Death in 1348, 1360, 1369, and 1375, local populations attacked Jews claiming that they had poisoned the wells.[33] So bad were the attacks and so widespread that Jewish historian Poliakov would liken 1347 to 1096.[34] Fueled by anti-Jewish rhetoric, Germans slaughtered Jews from no fewer than three hundred and fifty communities.[35] So many Jews were killed that in certain parts of Germany where Jews could no longer be found, Christians of Jewish descent, real or imagined, met the same end at the hands of the persecutors.[36] For a brief period after the plague had rescinded there was a move on the part of many princes to reinstate Jews. It was at this time that Jews became known for being traders in old clothes; no doubt there was a great surfeit of clothing as a consequence of so much death.[37] This in itself would not endear the Jews to their neighbors. But here is the beginning of something that would later feature in an embellished form, especially so in the eighteenth and nineteenth centuries: the Jewish peddler, who would become the visible appearance of the mystical Wandering Jew, the one who, having failed to help Jesus as he stumbled on his route to the cross, would be condemned to wander the world forever.

32. Poliakov, *The History of Antisemitism: Volume 1*, 111.
33. Stow, *Alienated Minority*, 239.
34. Poliakov, *The History of Antisemitism: Volume 1*, 109.
35. Goldhagen, *The Devil that Never Dies*, 84.
36. Goldhagen, *The Devil that Never Dies*, 112.
37. Poliakov, *The History of Antisemitism: Volumes 1*, 114.

Chapter 5

From Reformation to Enlightenment

THE THREE CENTURIES BETWEEN Reformation and Enlightenment were a mixed bag for Jews. The gradual wearing down of traditional religion and the growing criticism of age-old hierarchies created change in Western thought on an unprecedented scale. Luther's initial hopes of converting Jews had turned into writings that would become a blueprint for the Holocaust 400 years later, and Calvin's theocracy came to be seen as Christian nation in conflict with Christian nation, giving rise to skepticism on the merits of a religiously-led state. Greater interest in nature and the development of the sciences began to strip religion of its aura. By the end of the eighteenth century mythology was giving way to rationalism, divine inspiration to humanistic values, the supernatural to the natural world, and religion itself to science. Caught up in this extraordinary shift in thinking, it was thought that Jews would be liberated from the ghetto, become emancipated, welcomed into society, and valued by an increasingly secular world. But it turned out to be a false dawn as the old prejudices refused to die out on the streets and nationalism eventually reared its head in ways that would threaten the very existence of Judaism in Europe.

The impact of the Reformation upon European Jewry should not be underestimated. It was not just heretics that were burnt at the stake; anyone who seemed to be acting or believing in ways contrary to "God's will" had to be put to death. It was viewed as a dishonor to God to not do so. God's "wrath" somehow had to be satisfied by removing from the scene those who were in opposition to providence. Their continued presence was an indication that God's Laws were inexplicably contravened. Jews, with their reluctance to confess their "crime" and convert, were an obvious target.

As Calvinism swept across the states of central Europe it became more and more politicized; along with it went anti-Judaism (enforced by law) and all its abhorrent consequences. The linking of religion with the state and the subsequent wars helped give rise to a new view on society and government, one which promoted the possibility of separating the secular from the sacred. If God was the source of dispute, conflict, and war, then perhaps the states were better off without God. Couple this view in Lutheran areas with the two kingdoms doctrine and the foundations were already being laid for secular and not religious persecution, a persecution that would go unchallenged even by those Christians who might otherwise have stepped in. The old model of Christian monarchy reflecting the biblical as the ideal was slipping away; after all, as the secularists would argue, "look where that ended up: destruction and exile."

With his model for Biblical interpretation, Luther and his co-Reformers set off a train of thought that encouraged others to question whether the way things had always been thought and done was how they should remain. In the seventeenth century a number of thinkers began to ponder new ways of looking at the world and its order. One such person was Baruch Spinoza, a Dutch lens-grinder who is now recognized as one of the architects of the Enlightenment. Spinoza died at the age of 44 in 1677, probably as a consequence of inhaling glass filings that damaged his lungs. Raised in the Sephardi (Portuguese-Jewish) community of Amsterdam, he questioned the authenticity or reliability of the Hebrew Scriptures and is therefore viewed as the father of biblical criticism. It was this new level of scrutiny that would impact others and it was not long before his analysis would be embraced and developed in other fields of study, not least the understanding of revelation as presented in the Hebrew Scriptures. If this was not quite as it had been claimed then what else could stand the test of close examination? Whilst Luther and Calvin's focus on scriptural interpretation had led to new-found interest and regard for the Scriptures, Spinoza reduced their relevance. Even the view that love of neighbor was a divine instruction was questioned by Spinoza, claiming that Jews were only instructed to love members of their own religion and hate all others. Interestingly he cites Matthew's account of the gospel to "prove" his argument: "Love thy neighbor, and hate thine enemy." (Matt 5:43)[1]

1. Nirenberg, *Anti-Judaism*, 335.

Much of Spinoza's views could be summarized as follows: liberty of thought and conscience are prerequisites for any peaceful polity; the teaching of Jesus can only be limited to its context; revelation is not required for human blessedness; Jews are the enemy of reason as a consequence of their fixation with revelation.[2] He viewed himself as fulfilling the teaching of Judaism and therefore superseding it with his new "religion" of reason. Not only can we see this as the beginning of a whole new hatred building on the hatred of the past, but we can see how future forms of Jew-hatred could reinvent the past prejudices, finding new ways to say the old lies.

The fate of Jews during the seventeenth century was much the same as previous centuries: a sort of ebb and flow in fortune. For example, the Viennese emperor Leopold I who had been well-disposed toward Jews turned on them in 1669 after a series of unfortunate events for which the Jews unjustifiably got the blame, including a fire in the palaces and the empress miscarrying. Leopold's confessor asserted that these events must surely have been a warning from on high. The city's trading bourgeoisie saw an opportunity to rid themselves of the local competition and as a consequence the city was "free of Jews" for the next fifteen years.

It would not be the last occasion when Jews would be seen as competition in commerce; as economic revolution took hold across Europe this would become an increasing feature of Jew-hatred. Generally speaking Jews were in a prime position to capitalize on the situation. As we noted in an earlier chapter, Jews had been forbidden from owning land and were therefore city-dwellers confined to urban trades, including the much-maligned money-lending for interest. Christian agrarians tended to frown on such a role and thus held back economic growth, but Jews, excluded from the Guilds and their restrictive rules, were free to innovate and very much a part of economic progress. Advertising one's wares was another element that was frowned upon by Christian traders and artisans but Jews, keen to make what they could in difficult circumstances, were the first to promote their skills and goods in such a way. Because of the mobility of the communities, having been dispatched from city to city, state to state, over generations, the network that existed crossed borders and enabled Jews to profit from the movement of goods, exploiting upturns and downturns. Money, gold and jewels became the investment of Jews keen to avoid losing everything at the next pogrom or expulsion. What usury had also taught

---

2. As Christianity and Islam had each viewed Judaism as the "enemy," this particular claim would play straight into the hands of the proponents of anti-Judaism.

Jews was that fast turnover at little profit was a far better means of wealth creation than had earlier been the case; it is no coincidence that Jews tended to be the first to draw on mass production as a means of economic growth.

It was not long before Christian businesses began to complain of the competition, as seen earlier in Vienna in 1669. Similarly in Prussia, where the elector Frederick had invited fifty of the wealthiest Jew families in an attempt to revitalize the economy, pressure was soon exerted upon the state to ensure that Jews did not put Christians out of business. The only way to do that was with severe legislation; in order to keep the situation under control, poor Jews were hunted down and expelled.

This relationship between Frederick and the wealthy families along with other similar arrangements gave rise to the suspicion that Jews were deliberately working their way into the corridors of power. As a consequence, all Jews became the target of hatred from the rising bourgeoisie. Little consideration was given to the fact that the real power was in the hands of the rulers and indeed the churches to which they were affiliated; but the seeds of further discontent had been sown and would become impossible to uproot. Over subsequent centuries down to the present, the detractors claimed Jews to be wielding disproportionate power over society, government, and the world; as one rabbi friend of mine has said, "If only that were the case!"

The suspicion of Jews may have found yet another reason, one that was based on the old chestnut that Jews cannot be trusted because they tell lies: they had lied about their relationship with God by turning their backs on the covenant and they had failed to accept the Messiah, so why should they be trusted in commerce and power?

Despite all this, and in tandem with the growing understanding of the need for tolerance due to the lessening of respect for religion, emancipation became a real possibility. In 1781 Prince Charles de Ligne (1735–1814) claimed that 1800 years of oppression was long enough and that Jews should be free to live and have as many rights as anyone else.[3] The influence of Spinoza, John Locke, and others was spreading.

The Enlightenment would open up all sorts of possibilities for society while presenting many challenges for the prejudiced. It was inevitable that with the shaking of the old foundations of the Christian religion, the church's hold over society weakened. The liberalization of ideas and the increasing tolerance of those views that had once been deemed anathema

---

3. Poliakov, *The History of Antisemitism: Volume 3*, 31.

increased the possibility of freedom from the ghetto. Indeed the whole notion of deicide became not only questionable but even ridiculed in some circles, so why should the Jews remain in a permanent sate of victimization for a crime that could never have been committed? The mere existence of Jews despite 1800 years of persecution and massacre was surely testimony to the fact that they had something to offer the wider world.

Charles-Louis de Secondat, or Montesquieu (1689–1755), would come to see Judaism as the mother of both Christianity and Islam (in his terminology "Muhammedanism") but that each child had turned on her "stabbing her a thousand times."[4] He firmly believed that context and environment made people what they were, so if Jews were treated with greater tolerance they would become assimilated into society.[5]

A new dawn beckoned for European Jewry, perhaps one that had not been witnessed before. But it was to be a false dawn. Their detractors were still in existence not least in the person of François-Marie Arouet (1694–1778), known by his *nom de plume* Voltaire.

The fact that there was not a substantial number of Jews in France didn't deter Voltaire in his attacks upon them. His attacks on the church were not inconsequential either; he claimed Christianity to be little more than superstition. It was certainly not lost on him that what he was offering was every bit as much a revolution in thinking as that of Luther and Calvin 200 years earlier; whilst they attacked the Roman Church specifically, Voltaire attacked the church itself. What he and Luther shared in common was that in both cases the Jews ended up the target. More than 30 articles of the 118 in his *Dictionnaire Philosophique* were diatribes against Jews whom he called "the most abominable people on earth." Thankfully his hatred of Jews didn't sink to the depths of Luther's, and there was no repeat call to destroy synagogues and burn Jews. What did echo in Nazi Germany two centuries later was Voltaire's distaste for the Old Testament (Hebrew Scriptures); while admitting that it did have some positive features it nevertheless contained a lot of violence perpetrated by Judah and Israel on their enemies. This led to Voltaire's claim that Jews were little more than murderers.[6] French scholar Nicolas Fréret (1688–1749) claimed that the Hebrew Scriptures were an error leading to his view that Christianity too was an erroneous religion. His view was "Destroy the Jewish sect and Christianity

---

4. Poliakov, *The History of Antisemitism: Volume 3*, 80.
5. Nirenberg, *Anti-Judaism*, 51.
6. Nirenberg, *Anti-Judaism*, 357.

will collapse like a house of cards."[7] Such rhetoric was not dissimilar to earlier Jew-haters, nor would it be the last time such views would be expressed. Nazi Germany was certainly bent on a course to destroy Judaism before it turned on Christianity; its attempts to create a new church and religion is sufficient evidence of this claim. An English writer in the mid-eighteenth century, John Trenchard MP for Taunton, would write: "The terrible god of the Hebrews . . . A God of blood; it is with blood that he wishes to be appeased; it is with waves of blood that his fury must be disarmed; it is with cruelty that zeal for him must be evinced."[8]

Voltaire's Swiss contemporary Jean-Jacques Rousseau (1712–78) has a slightly better record. He viewed the three great monotheistic religions as competing faiths with little between them. However, according to Rousseau, it may be that the oldest was the best and the other two merely pale imitations. He considered Christianity to be the worst of the three since the church was wrapped up in persecuting those that disagreed with her tenets. Nevertheless he still had difficulty shaking off some of the old prejudices against Jews, as he believed the Jews to be base.[9]

Jews came to be seen as a test case for the doctors of the Enlightenment; if they were, as many believed, the most irrational of the human race and they were "converted to reason," then clearly the Enlightenment was going to supersede all the traditional religions. On the other hand, if they could not be convinced of the merits of the new ways of thinking and believing then they really were sub-human. Either way the Jews could not win. This logic bears not a little resemblance with that of Luther: convert or be condemned, damned if they did and damned if they didn't. Those Jews that did not assimilate as a consequence of eventual emancipation would therefore be cast aside as inferior, even non-human, not worthy of attention or care. Even if there were few physical attacks on Jewish communities in France during this period, the seeds were being sown for a new version of an old prejudice, this time under the guise of reason versus irrationality. From then on, theological and secular Jew-hatred would be singing from the same hymn sheet: convert or be condemned.[10] Indeed when France's National Constituent Assembly passed *The Declaration of the Rights of Man and Citizens* it came to be seen as superseding the Law given to Moses on

---

7. Poliakov, *The History of Antisemitism: Volume 3*, 117.

8. Poliakov, *Volume 3*, 122.

9. Poliakov, *The History of Antisemitism: Volume 3*, 100–102.

10. Nirenberg, *Anti-Judaism*, 350.

Sinai and numerous works of art depicted the *Declaration* on two tablets of stone.[11]

England, during this period leading up to the beginning of the nineteenth century, experienced a very different set of circumstances to those elsewhere in Europe. When Cromwell was petitioned to allow Jews to return after more than three and a half centuries since the expulsion of 1290, competition in trade was not such an issue. In the intervening years Christians had learnt to trade without Jewish involvement and had developed sufficient means by which the arrival of skilled Jewish traders posed little or no threat.

That is not to say that Jew-hatred did not exist: far from it. The writings of a Puritan by the name of William Prynne (1600–69) would argue that Cromwell was too soft on Jews and as a consequence Prynne printed a popular pamphlet that could be regarded as the first anti-Jewish material published in English in modern times.[12]

A century after the return of the Jews to England, the old suspicions resurfaced with an outpouring of anti-Jewish propaganda pamphlets. The catalyst for this was a bill, passed by both Commons and Lords in 1753, that merely allowed Jews to own land. The hostility was almost on par with medieval England and there was a real fear that massacres would ensue. Thankfully that was not the case, possibly due in part to the very low numbers of Jews in the country. But the climate was hostile and propaganda claimed that one day a Great Sanhedrin would install Talmudic Law over the land, with enforced observance of Shabbat, the banning of pork, and turning St. Paul's into a "Great Synagogue."[13] Pamphlets claimed that Jews were subjects of the devil, that there was a blackness beneath their eyes and were in perpetual hostility to Christ. The old tropes were peddled again, such as that Jews murdered Christians, and parish priests resorted to preaching the doctrine of persecution.[14] Tory opposition to the bill was an expression of orthodox high church Anglicanism that distrusted all things alien.[15] Some resorted to dragging out the claim that as the Hebrews remained Hebrew throughout slavery in Egypt so they would never be fully

---

11. Nirenberg, *Anti-Judaism*, 364.
12. Julius, *Trials of the Diaspora*, 249–50.
13. Poliakov, *The History of Antisemitism: Volume 3*, 37.
14. Julius, *Trials of the Diaspora*, 253.
15. Felsenstein, *Anti-Semitic Stereotypes*, 189.

incorporated into the life of English society.[16] It was not the first time, nor would it be the last, that their own history and Scriptures were used against Jews. In fact, one of the bill's opponents would argue that though Esau may have been prepared to sell his birth right to Jacob when he was hungry, the English were about to give away theirs for nothing.[17] There were even references to Mordecai's killing of Haman and 76,000 of his supporters as a warning that Jews would do the same to the English.

As a consequence of all the old stereotypes being employed, including that Jews are crucifiers, murderers, liars, and money schemers, tensions did rise to worrying levels and the bill was repealed just six months after it was passed. Church bells rang out across the land throughout the day as the news spread, bonfires were lit in places where Jews were probably never to be seen, and it was hailed as a great victory for the voice of the people.

Echoes of the past certainly resonate down to today, if not with regards to a Jewish conspiracy to rule the world, then in the fear of Sharia law being imposed by Muslims once they have taken over the great churches and government. One of the detractors of Jews in England at the time was the bishop of Gloucester, William Warburton (1698–1779), who expressed disbelief that God should have chosen such a vile race as the Jews, a theme that would be echoed two centuries later in the churches of Nazi Germany. The deists that had emerged in an earlier century began to lose their influence but their views remained an undercurrent in future prejudice, not least in the paganism of the Third Reich. Another echo from this period is how those that criticise Jews take on a morally superior tone. Later, this somewhat arrogant approach toward Jews became the chosen way of doing things in mid-nineteenth century England as debates ensued on whether Jews were deemed fit to sit in Parliament. But for now we concentrate on an earlier time when the seeds of later discontent were being sown.

One of the medieval myths with a claim to some Biblical authority resurfaced in eighteenth-century England: the story of the Wandering Jew. It had its origins in the belief that the Jew who struck Jesus during his interrogation by Annas[18] would be condemned for all eternity to wander the earth. The legend was popular throughout medieval Europe and whilst it

---

16. Sir Edmund Isham MP for Northamptonshire and quoted in Felsenstein, *Anti-Semitic Stereotypes*, 192.

17. William Northey MP for Calne and quoted in Felsenstein, *Anti-Semitic Stereotypes*, 197.

18. John 18:22–23.

was less frequently referred to in England it nevertheless became of some interest after the return of Jews under Cromwell. Like many other anti-Jewish myths, the tale of the Wandering Jew was able to adapt to changing circumstances. Because the English had for four centuries been denied any encounter with an actual Jew, the sight of a Jewish peddler was a cause for much excitement. The first to arrive in England had been wealthy merchants from Holland of Portuguese ancestry (Sephardi) but soon after poorer Jews from Poland and Germany began to arrive (Ashkenazi); these Jews scratched a living as itinerant salesmen. It was not difficult for them to soon be associated with the legend of the Wandering Jew, nor for tales to grow up around them that fostered hostility toward them.

In his only publication Henry Francis Offley would write in 1795: "The Son of God, who came into the world to purchase salvation to sinners (was) at length ignominiously crucified by the hands of the unbelieving Jews. But mark the result! The Almighty hurled down vengeance instantaneously on their heads, death and ruin to themselves and destruction to their country; hated by God, and despised by man, they were driven from society, and became vagabonds on the face of the earth."[19] As with the medieval period, questions as to why God would allow this to happen were easily explained by claiming that the Jews were an example of what happens when the wrath of God is incurred. Images from this period of the Jewish peddler or Wandering Jew would be a precursor to those featured in Der Stürmer, the weekly Nazi tabloid that was first published in 1923 and ran till the end of the Second World War. The typical caricature was of a Jew with a large hooked nose, darkened skin, piercing eyes and often with a hunchback. Despite the fact that there were no identifiable Jews in England at the time, Shakespeare was still able to draw upon people's fears and prejudices in his plays, the most notorious being through his character Shylock in *The Merchant of Venice*. Shylock is a bad man, manipulative and vengeful. The audience is invited to loathe him. This figure within English literature would echo through the ages and have a strong influence upon the English view of Jews. This view informed the depiction of Jews during the time we are considering and would continue to do so in the following century as the English novel became increasingly popular, not least Fagin in *Oliver Twist*. For many Britons the theatrical portrayals of Shylock and Fagin will inform how they view Jews in general.

19. Felsenstein, *Anti-Semitic Stereotypes*, 64.

Returning to the rest of Europe as we draw this chapter to a close, it would be remiss to not mention the impact of French Revolutionary campaigns. It is sometimes argued that the expansion of the French Republic led to the liberation of Jews from the ghettos of Europe. This is partly so. When Napoleon's forces took Venice in 1797 the Jews were freed from the ghetto restrictions for the first time in 281 years. As the French armies swept across conquered lands they took with them *liberté, egalité, fraternité*. But Napoleon was not that enamored by Jews and described them as "objectionable people, chicken-hearted and cruel."[20] Their allegiance to the Talmud was of serious concern for Napoleon and he hoped that through intermarriage the race would eventually die out. Like Cromwell before him he sought to draw upon the ancient model of government through the installation of a "Great Sanhedrin" which would link state and religious community in much the same way as it did 1800 years previously. In Napoleon's case, this stirred up antipathy amongst the people who feared that the Jews would begin some kind of takeover. The Great Sanhedrin lasted 28 days.

The Enlightenment was the culmination of three centuries of reform and increasing opposition to religious authority.[21] It was inevitable that Jews would welcome the first stirrings of liberation and eventual emancipation. But due to centuries of having contempt heaped upon them, many Jews remained disbelieving of any lasting progress.

The movement sought to put processes in place that were more rational than mythological, more humanistic than divinely-led, more akin to the natural world than the mythological, and more scientific than religious. So just as it attracted some Christians and was a source of anxiety for others, likewise in the Jewish communities: at what price freedom and equality? Assimilation could weaken the identity of Jewish communities and that which had bound them together for 1800 years. As well as giving them a reason to resist and survive, that identity could also be taken from them or, to be more accurate, be given up by them.

The Christian church, though losing some of its influence across Europe, sought to respond and recapture its hold over the governing authorities. This it did by becoming even more aligned with the state, despite the best efforts of the Enlightenment philosophers to break that link. Even if the church was no longer in the driving seat it was still in the vehicle, and a noisy passenger at that.

---

20. Poliakov, *The History of Antisemitism: Volume 3*, 226.
21. Fischer, *The History of an Obsession*, 40.

The old prejudices would not be buried for long; they were lying dormant just below the surface, in a state of hibernation, ready to rise and play their destructive role again in the longest hatred of them all.

"Neither the Enlightenment nor modernity overthrew the Christian theologies of Judaism . . . instead they translated them into new terms, embedding them in the philosophies and sciences with which they claimed to make a new and more critical sense of the cosmos."[22] This would remain true through successive movements into the future. The hate that is present in our world today has a long pedigree and even the promises afforded by the new dawn of the Enlightenment could not stop it morphing into a new form.

---

22. Nirenberg, *Anti-Judaism*, 301.

Chapter 6

The Emergence of Race and State

So far we have hardly mentioned the term "race" except to imply that the time was coming when we would have to. That time has now come. At the beginning of the nineteenth century race was rarely an issue, if at all, for the Judeophobes. By the end of the century it was the main reason given for vilifying Jews. Even if the hatred was less religion-based than previously it was no less vehement; indeed religious prejudice would rear its head and add to the hostility focused on Jews at regular and frequent intervals throughout the century. Such seemingly irrational behavior may have been fostered by fear of "foreigners" as nation states formed and empires were established, or it may have been a consequence of envy as emancipated, highly educated, and entrepreneurial Jews became successful in virtually all areas of life; but it must surely have had its roots in the hatred that had become deeply embedded in the human psyche after generations of contempt.

As the decades of the nineteenth century progressed, "race" became increasingly evident and over a few decades rose to be foremost in the Judeophobe's canon. As we have already noted, none of this was entirely divorced from the church. The traditional belief may have been that the human race descended from one couple, Adam and Eve, and evolved into differences due to family disputes, disinheritance, and dispersion, but new theories evolved that there was far more to it than that. Not content with a late eighteenth-century view that Africans were "sly, negligent and lazy," the Asiatic "gaudy and greedy" and the European "inventive and ingenious,"[1]

---

1. Carl Linnaeus (1707–78) quoted in Poliakov, *The History of Antisemitism: Volume 3*, 132.

Goethe (1749–1832) would develop the theme by arguing that Jews invented the view of Adam and Eve for their own ends. Goethe declared that holding the biblical couple to be the one from which all human beings were descended was a way of ensuring that Jews were seen to be the first and predominant race. It was, Goethe claimed, the way in which the world came to be subjected to the authority and governance of Jews. But according to Goethe, "Negroes and Laplanders" had very different origins.[2]

Johan Blumenbach (1752–1840) had already come to divide the human species into five distinct races based on research into skulls in 1779. But it would be grossly unfair to Blumenbach to lay any blame on subsequent claims by racists that this meant superior and inferior races. He could see no reason why poets of equal ability to their Parisian counterparts should not exist amongst the African peoples.[3] However, he did go on to suggest that as Jews had not interbred they retained certain characteristics that set them apart from their fellow Europeans, so much so he claimed that even laymen could distinguish a Jewish skull from any other.[4]

Within just a few decades the term "race" and its association with Jews became almost commonplace. Non-Jews now had another reason to propagate their hatred, not just a theological reason but an ethnological one: Jews were different not because God had set them apart but because they were a different race altogether, and an inferior one at that. Knowing of their difference, Jews chose to remain different to the exclusion of all others. The stage was being set for a catastrophe that would be like no other, an unprecedented assault on an entire race. Those that retained their allegiance to the Christian church believed that maybe God had all along ordained Jews to be different, and science was now merely confirming centuries of religious belief.

The full emancipation of Jewry not only in France but elsewhere across Europe was short-lived. It seems that despite all the progress made possible by more enlightened views, it was destined to be thwarted by old prejudices.

Leaving the ghetto, both physically and metaphorically, had both a positive and a negative impact upon Jews. Greater freedom often led non-Jews to believe that those they had persecuted for so long should become not only immersed but wholly assimilated into society. Taking on the full

2. Poliakov, *The History of Antisemitism: Volume 3*, 316.
3. Bendyshe, *Anthropological Treatises of Blumenbach and Hunter*, 312.
4. Poliakov, *The History of Antisemitism: Volume 3*, 139.

attributes and characteristics of a more secular society would inevitably lead to watering down the religious affiliation that had kept the Jews distinct and intact for centuries. It also began the long drawn-out debate as to whom Jews owed their allegiance, their religion and the scattered Jewish communities across Europe or the nation in which they were born or lived. In times of rising international tension, such an issue was not to be taken lightly.

On the other hand, because families had been dispersed across Europe in times of persecution and economic hardship, Jews were in an ideal position to capitalize on the rising new order of nation states and international trade. For those with long-established credentials and abilities in trade and money, Jews were able to benefit greatly from their position, transactions across borders, and the shifting of business dependent on fluctuating markets and economies.

Therefore emancipation brought a mixed reaction. Some Jews were happy to give up the ghetto, others were nervous about the new freedoms, preferring the physical and psychological "safety" of the ghetto walls.

As Jewish children were sent to public schools and mixed with non-Jewish pupils, as young Jewish men were conscripted into the military, and as Jews were no longer solely under rabbinic law but the civil courts, integration and eventual assimilation were well underway. The view that they would eventually become so integrated and assimilated that Judaism would die out was not without evidence and this actually led to some Jews becoming more entrenched in their mindset and for many led to a more conservatively religious reaction. It is clear that a more dangerous spiral was emerging, because alongside freedom for those that embraced it came entrenchment for others, and the more conservative they became, the more suspicion, fear, and hostility based on old prejudices would re-emerge.

As nation states were established, the conjecture rose that Jews were a state within a state, crossing international borders to engage in trade, communicating with other Jewish communities in the cities of opposing and hostile powers, speaking a common language alien to their country of residence and preferring to do so rather than engage with their immediate neighbors. Jews' preference to work with other scattered Jewish communities elsewhere in Europe helped ratchet up prejudice and exacerbate an already difficult problem. Divisions also arose within the Jewish communities with the assimilated being shunned by the more conservative, and correspondingly the increasingly wealthy Jews looking down upon those that remained traditional in their practice and belief. A later example of this could be seen when the long-established and more assimilated Jews of Berlin, who had won their rights and inclusion over many years, were hostile toward those Jews who, fleeing pogroms in the east, began to seek refuge in the city. Bringing residents of the *shtetl* into the cultured community of Berlin unnerved those Jews already present there; not only did these Jews not want to be reminded of their origins lest they be forced to slip back, but they also feared their rights would be eroded as a consequence of any adverse reaction by the non-Jewish population.

The hopes of those non-Jews that wished to see Judaism die out and the fears of religiously-traditional Jews were in part realised. By 1823 half of the Berlin Jewish community had been converted,[5] many seeking to better their prospects in commerce, the civil service, the judiciary, and the arts. But even this was not sufficient to ease the suspicions of many Judeophobes; indeed it was seen to be a reason for even greater fear. Some believed that the number of conversions was a Jewish conspiracy to deceive the world by infiltrating the Catholic Church.[6] The view that Jews are seeking to control the world through secretive organizations such as the Freemasons, the Illuminati and the deeply invidious and completely erroneous Protocols of the Elders of Zion persist to this day.

Releasing the constraints the church had put on society over the centuries was one thing, but what would come in its place was another. Shaking loose from religion through the adoption of reason and developments in science would usher in a whole new form of Judeophobia. This was an entirely new age and the old prejudice needed a new form of expression if it was to survive and continue peddling its myths and fostering its hatred.

French philosopher, socialist, and proto-Zionist Moses Hess (1812–1875), rebelled against the conservative Jewish beliefs of the household into which he was born; he would see this as the third great age. In his *Holy History of Man* Hess regarded the first age as that of God the Father, which began with Abraham and ended when Judaism broke up into sectarian strife. The second age was the Christian period of God the Son, which began with the life and teaching of Jesus. This second age was threatened by the inequalities that the Reformation sought to correct but failed to. The third age of modernity was ruled by God the Holy Spirit. According to Hess, this age was ushered in by Spinoza who had apprehended God with

---

5. Poliakov, *The History of Antisemitism: Volume 3*, 267.
6. Poliakov, *The History of Antisemitism: Volume 3*, 283.

his whole being. Reason and feeling were combined as never before into a comprehensive understanding of God and the purpose of life and history. It was the view of Hess that Jews were the inheritors of divine knowledge but had forfeited their spiritual legacy due to their inability to maintain equality.[7] Even this was to play into the hands of the Judeophobes, for they could argue again that Jews were not living up to their divine reason for being, so they were a failed people and no longer fit for their purpose. The French Revolution, the Enlightenment, and eventual emancipation all failed to live up to expectations. Dreams of an egalitarian utopia faded as the industrial age and capitalist societies took hold, with wealthy Jewish businessmen and bankers seen as the beneficiaries of inequality and purveyors of greed.

With a diminishing respect for religion amongst the upper echelons of society and in the corridors of academia, social and political action inspired by new secular philosophies ushered in new suspicions, fears, and prejudice. As the old structures fell, new ones came to be erected in their place.

Interest in ethnicity grew. It was not long before Jews came to be seen as an inferior race, not because of their religious beliefs or their inherited spiritual stain as a consequence of deicide, but simply because of their ethnicity. The trans-Atlantic slave trade had been maintained because Africans were not treated as humans but commodities in an increasingly-capitalistic world. William Lawrence (1783–1867) would write of black Africans as engaging in "disgusting debauchery and sensuality, and (displaying) gross selfishness."[8] It therefore did not take a leap of imagination to consider the possibility that other races were also inferior and it was not long before more immediate neighbors, namely the Jews, were seen to be not only racially different but inferior.

The roots of the Aryan myth, the belief that those of a particular European racial grouping were superior to other races and therefore a *"master race,"* were becoming embedded in the psyche of certain Judeophobes. In 1853 Richard Wagner (1813–1883) would come to believe that Judaism was so polluted that it had tainted early Christianity. The only way in which Christianity was to fulfil its calling as a religion of purity was to rid itself of its Jewish influences.[9] We shall come to read later that this would be

---

7. Barrer, *The Doctors of Revolution*, 501f.
8. Poliakov, *The History of Antisemitism: Volume 3*, 319.
9. Poliakov, *The History of Antisemitism: Volume 3*, 318.

played out again in one of the significant debates for the German churches of the 1930s as they considered dispensing with the Old Testament.

Wagner's paternity was questionable. He may well have grown up thinking that his mother had engaged in an illicit affair with a Jewish actor of which he was the product. Whether this is true or not, and whether this impacted him later in life, he certainly became embittered and a future icon for later Judeophobes. His relationship with a Jewish patron did not help matters, and Wagner came to believe that Jews were corrupt and that they dominated society by controlling both money and the arts. His hatred became obsessive and his work reflected that hatred; indeed his compositions would become the music of choice for many Nazis a century later. Many in the Nazi movement would regard him as a prophet and a forerunner to what was about to be unleashed on Jewish communities across Europe. European historian Robert Wistrich (1945-2015) in his sweeping work *A Lethal Obsession* wrote: "Wagner represents a crucial link between the Christian Judeophobic tradition and the 'redemptive' *antisemitism* of Nazism. His vision looked toward the future transformation of European man and the salvation of humanity through the radical solution of the 'Jewish question.'"[10]

A second "prophet" of what was to become National Socialism was a close friend of Wagner, German philosopher Friedrich Nietzsche (1844-1900) may have believed that Europe had much to thank the Jews for, and even that Zionism may have been the way forward, but he could not shake off the belief that Jews had some kind of supernatural power granted through their blood line. He even went on to suggest that Jews of some nobility should be selected to be assimilated into society. Over time, interbreeding with such Jews would enhance the master race. Where the Nazis diverged from his thinking was by the claim that they could find no one in the Jewish race suitable for such a program.

The pushback against the emancipation of Jews was already underway. This pushback was not based on religious prejudice but on race; this new expression of Judeophobia would even coin a new term, one that has come to be used as a catch-all for all forms of Jew-hatred, namely the term *antisemitism*. Even conversion or being non-religious would not be insurance against hostility; ancestry and ethnicity would be sufficient reason to be discriminated against.

---

10. Wistrich, *A Lethal Obsession*, 103.

In imperial Germany, the most popular author at the time was Gustav Freytag (1816–1895). His novels could be found in most households and therefore impacted the German psyche, even for those whom the church may no longer have had such an influence. In 1855 his book *Soll und Haben* (Should and Have), which was to be reprinted no fewer than 500 times, fostered racial hatred of Jews in a way that was to become very familiar through various works over the next decades, culminating in the vicious and vile publications of the 1930s and 40s. Freytag created two characters, one a non-Jewish German and the other a Jew. The former represented all that was good, the latter all that was bad. The novel as a form of media was now the means of spreading suspicion, fear, and hatred.

Freytag's English contemporary Charles Dickens (1809–1892) would not be immune to such prejudice. Almost twenty years before *Soll und Haben*, Dickens had created one of the most loathed characters in English literature: Fagin. Despite his protestations that he never meant any ill will toward Jews or their faith, Dickens could not escape the fact that he referred to Fagin's religious and racial origins no fewer than 257 times in the first 38 chapters of *Oliver Twist*. Once when he was challenged on this, Dickens stated that criminals on the streets of London were invariably Jews. In later editions Dickens himself removed one hundred and eighty references to Fagin's religious and ethnic roots.

Mention was made earlier that the term *antisemitism* was coined at this time. It is likely that Wilhelm Marr (1919–1904) was the first to use it in printed form in his 1879 book *The Way to Victory of Germanism over Judaism*. In it Marr argued that race had been at the heart of a longstanding conflict in Germany between Jews and non-Jews and that victory could only be accomplished through the total annihilation of one side by the other. It was Marr's view that the Jews were winning the battle and that their victory would bring about the death of Germans. As a consequence he formed the League of Antisemites and rallied like minds around him. The group was the first to focus on the alleged threat Jews were to German society and campaigned for their forced removal.

It would be insufficient to reason that Marr was merely a disturbed, angry, and bereaved man. It is true that he divorced his first and third wives and lost his second wife and their child through death within days of one another. It is also true that he claimed his Jewish employer had unjustly relieved him of his job. But there was so much more to it than that. As is often the case the social climate provided a framework for Marr's bitterness and hatred.

Marr was writing at a time of great social upheaval, and at the heart of the troubles was the increasing fear of the Jews. He fed off that fear. Thanks to the emphasis Jews had placed on the education of both genders, they were beginning to do very well across many disciplines, as we have hinted already. Once the state universities became open to Jewish entrants, it was not long before Jews had a much higher percentage ratio of their community in higher education than Protestant and Catholic communities.[11] Another factor was that as the stock market grew so too did Jewish involvement, and those Jews that did well in stocks and shares were more easily identifiable than non-Jews. As a consequence, Marr felt that religious arguments about Jews were petty compared to the real challenges evident in the socio-political changes that were taking place across Europe. Marr believed that an increasingly influential Jewish community could not be left to the theologians because Jews posed an existential threat to the state. The stock market crash of 1873 played straight into Marr's hands and Jews came to be seen by him and others as the only beneficiaries of the downturn. The old myth of wealthy Jews conspiring, scheming, and manipulating the economy for their own financial advantage came to the fore once again. Every economic crash since has led to similar claims, Wall Street and 2008 to name but two.

Prophecies of doom circulated: Europe would be brought to its knees while Jews rose to take control, and only then would a new Messiah, not necessarily the Christ but a savior of the people and nation, come along to rescue the people. Just 45 years later in the embers of the First World War such prophecies seemed to be coming true and it was not long thereafter that some felt their savior had come.

It was now patently clear that race was the prime reason for Judeophobia, hence the term *antisemitism*. Tragically, at the end of his life Marr sought to distance himself from the views he had earlier propagated. He rejected the view that Jews were the cause of social, economic, and political upheaval, citing the industrial revolution and rival political philosophies as the prime causes. He went on to beg pardon from the Jewish community for the damage he had done and feared that *antisemitism* was becoming linked with German nationalism and mysticism.[12] In this he may well have

---

11. Poliakov, *The History of Antisemitism: Volume 4*, 16.
12. Zimmerman, *Wilhelm Marr*, 154..

been a prophet all along, but the damage had been done and his contribution earlier in life to the growing hatred was probably irredeemable.

Classical Jew-hatred, namely that of anti-Judaism in the Christian church, was far from absent by the end of the nineteenth century but what was evident was that race had taken center stage. Jews were seen to be an alien race, a people apart. As noted earlier, as nation states became more firmly established, and borders more clearly defined, allegiance to the state in which one resided became more significant. For most people, living in what had been a fairly immobile society for centuries where travel was difficult and over generations a family might only have moved to the next village, this did not present a problem. But for Jews, often moved on from region to region, this was a serious issue. Not feeling as if they truly belonged to a place, having only arrived in living memory and with the extended family scattered across a wide area, Jews found their allegiance to a state under scrutiny. The German nationalist historian Heinrich von Treitschke (1834–1896) would not only distinguish Jews and Germans by their physical features, he would also raise fears of Jewish migrant traders from Poland whose children he believed would eventually take Germany over.[13] The seeds of nationalism were being well-watered in an increasingly fertile soil. *Antisemitism* was very much a part of the nationalist fervor and becoming more mainstream and acceptable across German society. Jews began to be excluded again from clubs and societies; the progress won through emancipation was being rolled back.

There is a very clear example of how the emancipation and assimilation of Jews into European society led to suspicion and hatred at the very end of the century. For twelve years from 1894 to 1906, this scandal in France occupied the minds of many and remains one of the most infamous miscarriages of justice in western Europe. Alfred Dreyfus was a young captain in the French artillery. In December 1894 he was convicted of treason and sentenced to life imprisonment after the authorities claimed that he had been passing military secrets to the Germans. Dreyfus, a French Jew with Alsatian ancestry, was incarcerated on Devil's Island in French Guiana. He was supported by many in the French *literati*, not least Emile Zola (1840–1902) in his open letter *J'accuse!* The case received much attention and in 1899 Dreyfus faced a re-trial. The affair divided French society and the sentence was commuted to ten years. However, it was later proven that

---

13. Poliakov, *The History of Antisemitism: Volume 4*, 21.

the allegations were unfounded and he was pardoned in 1906. Dreyfus returned to the army and served throughout the First World War.

Before this chapter closes we must recognize that as *antisemitism* reared its head across the European continent, Great Britain was not immune to it. The events in Tredegar, South Wales during August 1911 have been a source of debate amongst historians. Some claimed there was a pogrom, others that the destruction of shops owned by Jews was only another example of the rioting that had swept across the region at that time. My own view is that the British experience of pogroms being so limited gave rise to the misguided belief that this couldn't have been akin to those elsewhere in Europe. Thankfully no lives were lost. But the evidence is that a view had formed amongst the non-Jews that Jews in the town were opportunistically charging high prices and acting in dubious ways during a protracted coal mine strike. Only Jewish businesses were targeted in the assault. The violence spread through the Monmouthshire and Glamorgan valley communities. There are claims that Welsh hymns were sung as the shops were attacked accompanied by shouts of "let's get the Jews." Home Secretary at the time, Winston Churchill described the week-long attacks as a "pogrom." He sent members of the Worcester Regiment to impose military rule. For their protection Jewish families were evacuated to larger towns nearby. The Monmouthshire Welsh Baptist Association declined a formal resolution expressing sympathy for the Jews. It is reported that a number of ministers in their conference near Bargoed spoke against the move. One delegate warned that adopting such a resolution would only encourage more Jews into the area. Historian Geoffrey Alderman (b. 1944) is in no doubt that the events were religiously inspired along with "economically motivated prejudice."[14]

Whether the Tredegar violence was religiously, racially, or economically motivated, it was undeniable that racial prejudice had now become deeply entrenched in the European psyche. The view that Aryans were a superior race was now so prominent that a publication even claimed that Jesus was an Aryan.[15] The author, British-born German writer Houston

---

14. Alderman, "When the Pogrom of the Valleys Erupted in Wales."

15. Poliakov, *The History of Antisemitism: Volume 4*, 23. Commandeering Jesus was then, and remains today, part of the strategy in winning over people to the anti-Semitic cause. In the present, proponents of anti-Zionism will strip Jesus of his Jewishness and claim him to be a Palestinian. This is blatant nonsense but it is nevertheless an emotive ploy, with Jesus and Palestinians seen to be sharing their fate as victims of an occupying force.

Stewart Chamberlain (1855–1927), counted amongst his supporters the Kaiser, US President Theodore Roosevelt, George Bernard Shaw, and Leo Tolstoy. Such works playing on old religious prejudices and combining them with the new theories of race was a heady mix and a recipe for catastrophe. All it would take would be for a few events to conspire and bring it about.

Chapter 7

Edging Closer to Catastrophe

For those of us who were not there, our imagination has been fueled by newsreel footage, movies, poetry, and eyewitness accounts. We tend to conjure up darkness and cold, ice and snow, and the bitterness of winter. These images help us to begin the impossible task of comprehending something of the Holocaust. But they are insufficient. They will always be insufficient. Absolutely nothing can bring us close to the experience of one who has travelled for days in a cattle wagon packed with the anxious, forced out to a crowded platform, blinded by sudden light, and confused by those who seem to be pointlessly separating one from another. So we have made it black and white, cold and dark, rushed and chaotic. The truth is that yes, there were long nights, but there were long days too: the sun in clear blue skies, wildflowers splashing color in the hedgerow, birds singing at dawn, and people going about their business without a care in the world. For what did the disappearance of a neighboring family mean to them? This was the reality of the Holocaust: it happened in a world and a place just like ours. It wasn't always night, it wasn't always cold, it wasn't a black and white photograph. It was as we see the world today with people who had the same hopes and dreams as we have, the same fears and anxieties. It was as it is.

This thought came to me as I sat with my elder son on the train from Krakow to Oswiecim (Auschwitz) in 2012. It was my second visit to what has become the principal destination for those who wish to make a pilgrimage in commemoration of all that had taken place both there and in so many other death camps, forests, and quarries. Some of the buildings we passed would have been standing when train after train took people on the last leg of their final journey seven decades previously. The same trees swayed in the wind, summer flowers bloomed, and children played outside their homes. This was the reality, and it is a reality we hide from by presenting it in ways that so often safely deposit it in the past, in black and white, in darkness and cold, in chaos and noise. But as I get older the more I realize how recent it all was, how familiar that world is to my world, for it too was in color, it too required the appropriate clothing for the weather, and it too had an order beyond the uncertainty. The functionaries who operated the railway signals and those who serviced the locomotives were no different to the people I meet when I go about my life today; the victims were no different to the victimized today; in fact they can all be found in any generation of human life throughout history. We cannot name them, but we know them. This is the painful reality of the Holocaust. We were not there, yet we are. We are still, this very day, echoing the contempt of the past. Each new age has sought to address its past but it has never been enough. Somehow even when the horrors of recent years have demanded a rethink, the contempt has found a way through. On occasion it has re-formed so as to express itself in a surprisingly new way, but it is still the same contempt echoing the past. It is an evil vein pulsing with occasional malicious intent, but more often than not with an innocence that has a total disregard for the past. A failure to heed such a warning means the future may be just as bleak; after all, what makes us so arrogant as to believe we won't make the same mistakes that those who went before us made?

It was always my intention for this chapter to be the fulcrum of the book; how could it be any different? Judeophobia, in whatever its form, has its axis in the Holocaust. All expressions preceding 1933 when Hitler took up office inevitably draw us toward the catastrophe, and everything thereafter has as its shadow the Wannsee Conference,[1] the forests of Eastern Europe, and the gas chambers of Auschwitz.

Therefore this chapter has departed from the format of earlier chapters; it began with a reflection and it will end with a poem. German philosopher

1. Roseman, *The Villa, The Lake, The Meeting: Wannsee and the Final Solution*. The conference, lasting just a few hours, was held in January 1942 on the shores of Lake Wannsee, a short ride from Berlin. The delegates were some of the leading members of the Nazi Party, including Eichmann and Heydrich, who chaired the meeting. At the conference the logistics for the Final Solution were discussed and agreed. Millions of Jews were to be transported to death camps in the east. Mass murders had already been taking place but the genocide was to take a very different approach: the extermination of European Jewry was to become industrialized, drawing on the most effective economical means possible.

Theodore Adorno (1903–1969) is often quoted as saying, "after Auschwitz there can be no poetry." This is an inaccurate translation; what he actually said was *nach Auschwitz ein Gedicht zu schreiben, ist barbarisch*: "To write a poem after Auschwitz is barbaric."[2] Yet how else, other than through poetry and art, can we who were not there dig deep enough into our being to even begin to glimpse something of the horror? This is why I began this chapter with a reflection and will end this chapter with a poem; a mere analysis of the descent into the evil that was the Holocaust is insufficient; it demands so much more of us. Even this cannot do justice to what took place but it has the intention of paying respect. This book is merely an attempt to log the phenomenon that is Judeophobia, how it has mutated with the times, and how the church has been at the heart of its formation and expression. So we cannot, for now, do much more than touch upon the issues and the characters pertinent to our study. What will become clear is that although there have been many genocides before and after the Holocaust, it was unprecedented both in its scale and its method. To claim some kind of equivalence with other genocides does neither the Holocaust nor the other genocides any respectable service. Indeed today's Judeophobes, in the form of anti-Zionists, try to discredit the State of Israel by calling the Naqba, or even the situation in Gaza, a "holocaust." As we have already seen from our brief overview of the history of Judeophobia this form of slur has been reinvented time and again, blaming the Jews for something they themselves have suffered, often on a far greater scale.

So let us begin at the first half of the twentieth century and how the anti-Judaism of the Christian church played into the hands of those who wanted to rid Europe of its Jews. It was Edmund Burke (1729–1797) who wrote "In order for evil to flourish, all that is required is for good men to do nothing." This is true, but the Holocaust has taught us another lesson and it is this: in order for evil to flourish, all that is required is for good people to make the wrong choices. Many good people not only stood by, but many also participated in the greatest crime in the history of humanity. How could this be?

As mentioned at the end of the last chapter, by 1900 racial prejudice had become so deeply entrenched in the human psyche that for many Germans the belief that the Aryan race was superior to all others was almost a given. Even Jesus was to be portrayed as an Aryan, because how else could one understand his genius? A blond-haired, blue-eyed Jesus adorned many

2. Franklin, *A Thousand Darknesses*, 2.

a Sunday School classroom in Britain well into the late twentieth century. I sometimes call this image the "Lake District Jesus," with Disney-type animals fawning around his feet and a very European landscape in the background. But the Aryan Jesus was no laughing matter for the Jews of Europe as *antisemitism* took hold. It was an expression of the contempt in which they were held by their non-Jewish neighbors. The commandeering of Jesus was and remains a useful act in seeking to win over those not previously committed to the Judeophobic cause. Today anti-Zionists also like to strip Jesus of his Jewish ethnicity and choose to claim him as a Palestinian instead, a victim of an occupying force.

Jesus was not alone in being targeted by the Judeophobes. At the beginning of the twentieth century it was becoming more acceptable to question the origins of the Old Testament, the Hebrew Scriptures. Biblical criticism had reached such a level of scrutiny that sources of Mosaic Law began to be debated as never before. As the biblicists concluded that much of the Pentateuch had been compiled from a range of material during the Babylonian exile, the authenticity of Judaism itself became of interest. Maybe it was just an amalgam of ancient Middle Eastern religions after all, and the Jews were no more special than any other people. Further study of ancient Egyptian texts led to the understanding that even the Law had not been given to Moses on Sinai but was an appropriation of Egyptian moral codes. This may be so, but in the hands of the Judeophobes such knowledge was pure dynamite; it would help endorse the belief that Jews were merely doing what they have always done: engaging in theft and deception.

The provenance of the Hebrew Scriptures would play a significant role in the delegitimizing of Jews and Judaism with the rise of the Nazi Party and the response of the churches. Both the socio-political roots of National Socialism and the theological roots of what would become church complicity in the Holocaust were becoming firmly established. Alongside similar writings, the Austrian magazine *Ostar* urged Aryans to exterminate "apemen" (Jews). These articles were being read by impressionable young men such as Hitler and Himmler.[3] Violence against Jews in Germany had been sporadic during the previous century with riots in 1830, 1834, 1844, and 1848 and the seemingly last flurry of religious hostility came with twelve ritual murder trials between 1867 and 1914 (all but one ended in acquittals). The Catholic theologian August Rohling (1839–1931) teaching in the University of Prague was perhaps the most vehement of the religious

---

3. Poliakov, *The History of Antisemitism: Volume 4*, 28.

detractors; his views may have been discredited by more capable theologians but nevertheless he helped influence Catholic thinking and some priests would filter his views down to the pew.[4] Such attacks, however, could not be compared with what was going on in Russia at the time. Pogroms, in particular those following the assassination of Tsar Alexander II in 1861, meant that thousands of Jews fled west—causing further tensions in Germany, as mentioned in chapter 6.

The outbreak of war in 1914 seemed to bring the Germans together. Whatever their ethnicity or religion, they rallied round a common cause. For the very first time, Jews were permitted to serve as officers in the German military. A quarter of a century later this merely added to the confusion of Jews when they could not understand why their war service, and in many cases their heroism, did not protect them from persecution and transportation.

However, even at the time common service in defence of the fatherland during the First World War didn't remove the prejudice altogether. In 1916 a census was held to determine how many Jews were serving in the military. This came about as the anticipated swift victory was not being realised and Jews again became the inevitable scapegoat. Rumors began circulating that Jews were shirking their duty and avoiding service in the military. Whether the census was going to be used to prove or disprove such rumors we cannot say; nor will we know for sure whether it did or did not, as the results were never published. However it is strongly believed by analysts that Jews were as much at the front as any other group within Germany.

Not only did German Jews find themselves serving alongside their non-Jewish countrymen on the front line, and indeed in officers' quarters, but a Jew was appointed to one of the most significant roles in the German Government. Businessman Walter Rathenau (1867–1922) was given the responsibility of managing the allocation of Germany's limited raw materials to the war effort. However, both Rathenau's involvement at this level and the nature of the work he was engaged in, together with the involvement of Jewish businesses in the war effort, merely added to the *antisemitism* of the early post-First World War years. The belief that Jews were the main financial beneficiaries of the war tapped into the prejudices of the past, including that Jews always managed to cash in on human catastrophe.

---

4. Poliakov, *The History of Antisemitism: Volume 4*, 16.

What is true is that Jews were "punching above their weight" in the years after the war. Even though they formed just 1 percent of the German population, 75 percent of them were engaged in white-collar jobs in commerce, banking, medicine, and the law; Jews owned 40 percent of Germany's textile firms and 60 percent of clothing businesses. Most of these were very small businesses so the statistics can hide the reality somewhat, but it is a fact that some of the largest department stores were owned by Jews and almost half the private banks were in Jewish hands.[5] All of this contributed to the age-old fear of "creeping control" over the economy and that at some point in the future non-Jews would be completely beholden to Jews—a fear that was as unfounded as it was ridiculous. But reason is often the first casualty in such prejudice. Another myth was that Jews continuing to have large numbers of children in each family meant that they would soon take over Germany. A number of factors behind a drop in the birth rate at the time was firstly improvement in child mortality owing to developments in medical science, and secondly the need to avoid large numbers of children in a family because of the parlous state of the economy; a reduction in pregnancies was made possible by the availability of improved birth control. For the Judeophobes the fact that Jews continued to have large families posed an imagined threat to the existence of Germany. This fear was deepened with the Jews from the east, who tended to have larger families than their often more assimilated and settled coreligionists. These Jews rarely occupied middle-class roles and were more often than not in the poorer strata of society. Having fled persecution and pogrom they now found themselves up against more sophisticated forms of prejudice, but it was prejudice nonetheless. In the east they had faced religious persecution, but in Germany a developed form of racism would make life difficult for them. They were especially exposed to exploitation whilst seeking citizenship; it was both an extraordinarily complicated and a protracted process. Non-Jews were unlikely to engage them in work because clients would soon begin to boycott their business. Boycott would become an increasingly frequent tool of the racists, not only of Jewish businesses but of those non-Jewish businesses that worked with Jews.

The challenging citizenship process coupled with the boycotts meant that many Jews were mostly unemployable and therefore deeply vulnerable. Despite the claim made by the anti-Semites that the Jews did well out of the Wall Street Crash and subsequent Depression, the fact is that living

[5]. Poliakov, *The History of Antisemitism: Volume 4*, 12–13.

standards for Jews dropped as considerably as any other ethnic or religious grouping; Jews were and are no more immune to economic downturn and poverty than anyone else.

The fate of Rathenau was emblematic of the fate of the Jews in the early years after the armistice. Just as the fortunes of Jews had been tied to the progress of the Enlightenment and emancipation, so too would they be tied to any negative reaction to it. When the guns fell silent over the fields of Belgium and northern France, shock settled upon the minds of the exhausted German public. That shock would turn to shame, anger and scapegoating once the Versailles Treaty impacted them. Rathenau, who had seen it as his patriotic duty to manage the scarce natural resources in Germany, then became a high-profile hate-figure of the far right. Mistrust of the newly established Weimar Republic by the church as well as by the judiciary, academia, civil service, and even the military (dented but not diminished in influence across German society) added to the problems for the government. In 1922 after serving as minister of reconstruction, Rathenau faced the enormous task of being appointed foreign minister—though even his mother opposed it. He accepted the post as he believed they could not find anyone else to do it; such was his sense of duty and his belief that by doing so he would help break down the barriers created by *antisemitism*.[6] Rathenau sought to build bridges with the former enemies of Germany, which merely poured fuel onto the flames of hatred. It was even claimed that he had deliberately sabotaged the war effort in order to benefit from the armistice. Rathenau faced vile personal attacks from his political opponents even within the Reichstag, while crowds outside called for his death.[7] His murder on June 24, 1922 was the 345th political assassination by right-wing extremists since the war. A little later in the year a professor of math at Heidelberg published figures detailing political killings since the war. The figure had risen to 352 by the right wing extremists and 22 by the left. Interestingly, the professor noted that the leftists had received convictions totaling 248 years imprisonment while the right received only 90 years in prison and 730 marks in fines.[8] Such was the disparity and indeed climate under which the moderates in Germany were trying to operate.

The Weimar Republic had offered Jews the chance to contribute to German society as never before. As it began to fall apart, so too did the

6. Elon, *The Pity of It All,* 363.
7. Elon, *The Pity of It All,* 370.
8. Elon, *The Pity of It All,* 368.

fortunes of the Jews. The modernism of the Republic's early years had been swift and disorientating. Germany was a far different country in the 1920s than it had been just two decades before. This left many ordinary Germans bewildered and concerned. It seemed to some, especially Calvinistic Protestants, that a moral malaise had set in and there was a real fear that everything would spin out of control; it would, but not in the way that was expected. The backlash when it came was overwhelming.

Many of us may wonder how the church was to play a significant role in the rise of Hitler and the implementation of his policies. But play a role the church did: in part it was indifferent and in part it was active in the war that was waged against Jews. To amend the earlier quote, all it took for evil to succeed was for good people to make the wrong choices. Remaining silent was tantamount to complicity, but making the wrong choices and actively pursuing anti-Jewish policies was nothing less than collusion. All too few in the church could act any differently, not just because they weren't able to withstand the likely consequences but because most were simply unable to see wrong from right. The Jews had been the focus of church contempt for centuries so why should anything change just because the newly-elected Nazi government had decreed they be persecuted?

It is often claimed that Chinese Premier Zhou Enlai (1898–1976) quipped in 1972 that it was too soon for the consequences of the French Revolution to be fully understood. The truth is that he probably misunderstood the question owing to a translation error during President Nixon's visit to the country and was actually referring to the more recent turbulence of 1968. Nevertheless it has come to be useful in recognizing that major historical events have consequences long into the future; for example, we could probably argue that the impact of the First World War didn't end in a railway carriage with the signing of the armistice but with the fall of the Berlin Wall 70 years later. So it is that we still cannot fully appreciate the impact of the Holocaust on philosophy or theology. What we can do is seek to examine the debates and actions of the Christian church during that time in the hope of learning from history. For this to happen we have to be honest and open to the possibility that the church simply got it wrong, badly wrong. If the Holocaust was catastrophe for European Jewry then it remains a stain on the Christian church. Only close examination of the error of the church, admission of guilt and, to draw on a theological term, full repentance will allow the church to come to terms with what it has done in contempt toward the Jews, not only in Germany over the twelve years of the Third Reich but over the course of its history.

In the days after the fall of Berlin, newsreels relayed images from the concentration camps. Christians across the world inevitably asked where the church in Germany had been in all of this; it couldn't be, surely, that the church had allowed this to happen without significant protest. Tragically, the truth is that it did. The evil that was the Final Solution went virtually unchecked and it cannot be denied that six million Jews were rounded up, transported, and selected by, in the main, baptised Christians.

The church had to find heroes of resistance. It was understandable that it should turn to Lutheran theologian Dietrich Bonhoeffer (1906–1945). Famously executed in Flossenbürg concentration camp just a month before the German surrender, Bonhoeffer had been convicted of being party to the attempt on Hitler's life in the plot of July 20, 1944. He was one of the Nazi regime's fiercest critics with a sharp intellect and a courage that was rarely surpassed. In the post-war period his writings would become revered and his theology in an age of change and secularization offered a significant contribution to the debate as to how the church could respond. However, it is only in recent years that time has provided sufficient distance to afford the opportunity of presenting a fuller account of Bonhoeffer's views during the Nazi years. On closer and more objective examination, away from the understandable and rightly concluded view that Bonhoeffer was a martyr, it becomes possible to detect that Bonhoeffer also had a strain within his theology that can provide a warning to the contemporary church.

Born into a family that was politically on the left, and one that rarely attended church except for the main festivals, Bonhoeffer would grow up in an environment that was somewhat different to his Lutheran colleagues. It may well be that having not been so exposed to the anti-Jewish views of most sermons and Biblical exposition, his Judeophobia was less evident. Nevertheless, his theological education established within Bonhoeffer the traditional view of Jews being responsible for their own suffering: having rejected the Messiah and put him to death, Jews were condemned to eternal blame. As a Christian pastor, Bonhoeffer could not be completely immune from centuries of church contempt.

Opposition to Hitler ran in the family, not from a theological but a political standpoint. His brother met the same fate as Dietrich, so too did the husbands of two of his sisters. It was these two factors, politics and a limited exposure in his early years to church Judeophobia, that set Bonhoeffer apart from the vast majority of his contemporaries. In addition Bonhoeffer travelled more widely than most. Travelling beyond their borders was pretty rare in the interwar years for Germans still reeling from being defeated in 1918. Bonhoeffer was not especially liked amongst his colleagues partly as a consequence of his travels, for many frowned upon anyone who was seen to be "fraternizing" with the former enemies that had so damaged Germany at Versailles.

There is no doubting Bonhoeffer's integrity and courage, as few were as bold as he in criticizing the Nazi state. But, like the vast majority of his colleagues, virtually nothing was said by him in defence of religious Jews. Not only was historic Judeophobia part of Bonhoeffer's psyche but it is evidenced in his writing. He had no qualms about using the term "the Jewish problem;" in other words he was willing to accept that there was such a thing as an issue. He would also draw on the two kingdoms doctrine of the Lutheran Church to avoid engaging in criticism of the state in its anti-Jewish legislation; the fate of the Jews was in the hands of authorities appointed by God. Bonhoeffer was clearly unwilling, or even unable, to recognize that centuries of suffering were actually caused by a church that was predisposed to punish and persecute an entire people for the perceived actions of their ancestors, a perception that was wholly wrong in that it had been politically conceived.[9]

Bonhoeffer was far from being alone in this. When Christian leaders met in Barmen in 1934 to draw up a declaration to oppose Nazification of the churches there was no criticism of the Nazis' beliefs and actions against the Jews. Some commentators seek to excuse this omission by claiming it was to make the declaration as widely acceptable as possible, but the more likely reason was that mistreatment of Jews was not at the forefront of the delegates' minds. A year earlier, Bonhoeffer had expressed some sympathy for Jewish suffering and went on to state that it was the government that had the responsibility for dealing with "the Jewish problem." As a young theologian Bonhoeffer's view was less significant than that of the silence of the Barmen delegates. The fact that the Barmen Declaration uttered not a single word in defence of Jews gave the state almost free range in developing its anti-Jewish program. The Nazi regime must have become convinced it could now operate free of church criticism because the two kingdoms

---

9. Ericksen, *Complicity in the Holocaust*, 35.

doctrine meant that it was merely acting within its God-given authority.[10] Within a year the Nuremburg Laws came into effect.

The Nuremberg Laws redefined what it was to be a Jew under German law. The term no longer referred to a person's religion but formalized the view that had been developing over decades, that "Jew" was a term that defined ethnicity. The Nazis now determined a Jew to be anyone with three or four grandparents that were Jewish. This legislation therefore brought under the cloud of persecution many more people than was the case before. Even if grandparents had converted to Christianity, it was not enough to afford protection from the Nazi wrath. Many Christians who thought themselves immune now found themselves discriminated against, pastors amongst them. It was these that some Lutherans, Bonhoeffer included, sought to defend. If there was any resistance to speak of from the Lutheran pastors and theologians with regards to the onslaught against Jews, it was on behalf of those with Jewish ancestry and not those that continued to practice their Jewish faith.

I can't recall when I first became aware of the Holocaust. I couldn't have had one of those heart-stopping experiences when the horror suddenly became known to me, otherwise I would surely have remembered it. Maybe as someone who, from childhood in the 1960s, has been interested, fascinated even, by the Second World War, the Holocaust became so gradually known to me that I only slowly became alert to the gravity of the catastrophe. Meeting survivors of the camps, members of the kinderstransport, and someone from the MS *St. Louis*[11] ten years into my ministry drove home something of the nightmare that enveloped and almost wholly destroyed European Jewry. I wondered how I would have fared as a victim of Nazi oppression. At that stage I was not quite as fit and active as I had been, and being the father of two young boys I would have definitely been separated from them and my wife. My guess is that I would not have survived long. But then I began to wonder, what if I had been on the other side of the race divide? Would I have been a perpetrator, a rescuer, or a bystander? Whilst I would have liked to have seen myself as a rescuer, I

---

10. Ericksen, *Complicity in the Holocaust*, 100.

11. The MS *St. Louis* was a German ocean liner that that carried nine hundred Jewish refugees from Nazi Germany across the Atlantic in search of haven. Despite assurances that they would be accepted as refugees, the passengers were turned away from Cuba, the United States, and Canada. After returning to Hamburg some found respite in Belgium, the Netherlands, France, and Great Britain. Around a quarter of them eventually perished in the camps.

somehow doubt that I would have been. Many years later I came to discover that amongst the trees that commemorate the Righteous Amongst the Nations[12] at Yad Vashem, Israel's Holocaust memorial, there are just three Methodists represented: Henryk and Maria Hoffman and Władysław Kołodziej, and all three resided in Poland.

Henryk Hofman had already fallen foul of the Nazi occupiers by refusing to sign the *volksliste*, a form of census that classified those in occupied lands into categories of desirability. But being of German ethnicity, Henryk was also mistrusted by his Polish neighbors. Henryk and his wife Maria sheltered and fed, without reward and in great danger to themselves, a Jewish family in their home near Warsaw from the autumn of 1943 until the German retreat in the face of the Russian advance. Zygmunt Szaniawski had arrived at the Hoffman's door pretending to be a Polish officer seeking help for him, his wife, and daughter. The Hoffmans realized that the family was Jewish and it is reported that it was their Methodist beliefs that led them to fulfill the request. After the war the Szaniawski family migrated to Israel and kept in touch with the Hoffmans; each visited the other over a number of years. The Hoffmans were recognized as Righteous Among the Nations in 1991.

Kołodziej also had a reputation for resistance before he too participated in the rescue and shelter of Jews. In 1935 Polish nationalists had been planning a pogrom against the Jews of Brest Litovsk; this was foiled by Methodist minister Kolodziez. During the occupation Kołodziej was living in Krakow and was part of the underground resistance. A number of Jews, some escaping the ghettoes, found him to be a source of great help. Locating safe houses and even sheltering Jews in his own home, Yad Vashem records that Kołodziej had been guided by his Christian love and compassion and was recognized as Righteous Among the Nations in 1980.[13]

Even taking into account the fact that Methodists across continental and Nazi-occupied Europe were small in number, the fact that only three are so recognized by Yad Vashem leads me to question how I, as a Methodist minister, would have responded to a knock at the door by a Jew in need of help when the dangers to not only myself but my family were great.

---

12. A tree is planted to honor a non-Jew who acted without gain or favor in the rescue of a Jew from the Holocaust.

13. Righteous Among the Nations Department, Yad Vashem, the World Holocaust Memorial, Jerusalem.

It was after meeting and getting to know a German veteran who had fought in the Ukraine that I began to fear that I could easily have been swept up in the fervor that accompanied Hitler's election. As a twelve-year-old boy, the veteran heard an elderly woman tell his mother on the street in Berlin where he lived that if Hitler was elected the next day they may as well all be buried alive. He was understandably terrified. But then, the veteran told me, the balconies had party banners hanging from them, spring flowers began to bloom, the pavements were cleaned, and people held their heads high in expectation. He had never known his city to be so hopeful and happy. At eighteen he enlisted. The rest of his testimony became cloudy. He recounted just two incidents from the eastern front. The first was coming under an attack that killed one comrade and wounded another; the second was entering a village to be welcomed by villagers with hot drinks and bread. Such hospitality bewildered him because he felt sure the hosts believed they were about to be killed. He informed me that on capture he had hastily removed his insignia. Sitting with someone who was so likeable, a proud Christian who was devoted to the study of Scripture, brought home to me the very real possibility that I might not have been a rescuer, nor a bystander, but a perpetrator.

As mentioned above, there have been just three Methodists awarded the honor of being Righteous Among the Nations, but there are plenty of Methodists who willingly served in the SS. Indeed a large number of Methodist ministers were members of the Nazi Party. As a Methodist minister myself I find this terrifying, as I am not sure how I would have stood against the pressure to conform to the mood of the age. Would I have seen that the Nazis' actions were morally wrong and that it would end in disaster? Or would I have believed, as many Methodists believed, that Hitler was the savior of the German people?

What was shocking for me was the moment I realised that the Methodist Church in Germany had been actively supportive of Hitler and the regime. I had grown up thinking of the church to which I belonged as being tolerant toward people of a faith different to our own, courageous in standing up to the oppressor, and engaged in the pursuit of social justice and scriptural holiness. What on earth went wrong in Germany during the 1930s that all of this went out of the window? It seems to me that only by trying to find an answer to this perplexing question can we even begin to address the theology and practice that we have referred to throughout this book, namely the contempt with which the Jewish people have been held. If it affected those in my denomination as recently as in living memory, just a decade or so before I was born, then how far have we come in tackling the issues, beliefs, and practices that have been so much at the core of Judeophobia over two millennia? My fear is that we have not got very far at all, as I will evidence in chapter 8. But for now, let us remain focused on 1930s Germany and spend some time examining the collusion of the Methodist Church in the actions and maintenance of the Nazi regime.

There is very little published in English about the Methodist Church in 1930s Germany. By far the best article, so far as I am aware, is the very thorough one by Seventh-Day Adventist academic Roland Blaich entitled "A Tale of Two Leaders: German Methodists and the Nazi State."[14] It makes salutary reading. Blaich compares the responses of the two leading European Methodists at the time: German-American John Nuelsen (1867–1946), bishop of the Europe Central Conference of the Methodist Episcopal Church which included Germany; and Otto Melle (1875–1947), who was elected bishop of the German Episcopal Church when it became more independent of the Central Conference in 1936.

In the spring of 1933, shortly after Hitler had become the Fuehrer, Nuelsen was invited by Propaganda Minister Josef Goebbels and the Foreign Minister Konstantin von Neurath to visit prisons to ensure that political prisoners were being treated fairly. Happy to oblige, Nuelsen was able to report favorably on the conditions in which the prisoners were kept. He did so with the leader of the Lutheran Church, Otto Dibelius, via a radio broadcast to the United States and encouraged his superintendents to send telegrams to Britain and the US, asking them to stop criticizing the new government.

Later in the year Nuelsen toured the United States with the message that the change of government had been affected without bloodshed and that Germany had a bright future. He did so again in 1935. He claimed that nowhere on the European continent were Methodist Churches as free as they were in Germany. The restrictions placed upon and the conflicts within the Lutheran Church were not impacting Methodists. After all, the Lutherans were part of a state church and therefore it was understandable that the new government wished to have a say in their restructuring.

Residing in Switzerland and more rooted in America than his colleagues Neulsen took a slightly more objective view than they—and after a while he began to have doubts about the intentions of the regime. With

14. *Church History* 70 (2001) 199–225.

hindsight we might have expected this sooner but for the euphoria surrounding the new regime. This was certainly evidenced in letters and editorials in the British weekly *The Methodist Recorder*; there are far more letters explaining away the situation in Germany as a consequence of Versailles and subsequent events than expressing concern for the plight of the Jews. Indeed a number of letters from German Methodists sought to reassure anyone who dared question the motives of the Nazis.

Not so influenced by the two kingdoms doctrine as his German colleagues, Nuelsen would counter Rom 13:1: "Let every person be subject to the governing authorities for there is no authority except from God, and those authorities that exist have been instituted by God," with Matt 20:25–34:"You know that the ruler of the Gentiles lord it over them, and their great ones are tyrants over them. It will not be so with you."[15] Nuelsen was therefore not to be so intimidated by the Nazis. Despite expressing some positive things about the change of government he would still retain concerns; writing to American bishops as early as 1933 he described the regime as "a ruthless and unscrupulous dictatorship." Despite the fact that he wanted to retire in 1934, he stayed on out of a sense of duty because he didn't wish to create the impression that he agreed with the regime. However when the German Methodists broke away from the Central Conference in 1936 Melle was to become their leader. Nuelsen would issue a *cri de coeur* on the election, urging the church to obey God's word and raise its voice should the regime act in ways that were manifestly anti-Christian.[16]

Melle was an altogether different character to Nuelsen. Less academic and more of an activist, Melle saw Hitler as divinely appointed. Nuelsen wrote that Melle believed that the new religious stirrings in Germany were "the greatest event to have happened in the last 2000 years." His assessment of Melle was accurate.

Prior to his election as bishop of the German Methodists, Melle made an extensive tour in 1935 of universities and churches across the United States. In his lectures he spoke of the benefits of the Nazi laws on eugenics and on Nazi achievements since coming to power, not least the reduction in unemployment and the cleaning up of society. The latter was a significant factor in German Methodist approval of Hitler; pornography had been removed from newsstands, plays at the theater had been cleaned up, and the fact that Hitler was teetotal also helped win the admiration of Melle and his

15. Blaich, "A Church in Crisis."
16. Blaich, "A Church in Crisis."

colleagues, as well as Hitler's high regard amongst the youth of Germany. Melle would even speak in favor of people being sent to concentration camps for selling "salacious material."[17] According to Melle, his message went down well with the young people. All his expenses for the tour were met by the German Foreign office and the National Health Committee together with a 6,000 Reichsmark donation from someone who wished to be anonymous. Clearly Melle was a serious player in the Nazi propaganda machine.

The next key moment in Methodist support for the regime came in 1937 when more than 400 delegates from 45 countries gathered for a major ecumenical conference in Oxford.[18] Up until the last few days before the conference, it was believed that the Nazis would not permit any church leaders to attend. Indeed none of the invited Lutherans or Reformed did, the highly regarded Pastor Martin Niemöller (1892–1984) amongst them. However, not surprisingly Melle along with two colleagues arrived with the full support of the regime. It is clear from the records of the occasion that Melle and his Baptist counterpart Paul Schmidt were keen to present a positive picture of Hitler and the activities of the Nazi government, and also to challenge any moves to criticise them. When concerns about the regime were expressed by the delegates it was agreed that a letter be drawn up and sent to the German government.

There were five points made:

1. That in view of their extensive work and involvement in the preparations for the Conference, it was deeply regretted that no one from the German Evangelical Church was present.

2. That the delegates were aware of the afflictions of "many pastors and laymen" in Germany.

3. That they were also aware that the oppression being experienced by the German Evangelical Church was also being inflicted on the Roman Catholic Church.

4. That they were all members of the "body of Christ" in the world, and therefore as the German churches suffered, Christians throughout the world suffered with them.

---

17. Blaich, "A Tale of Two Leaders," 201.

18. The Oxford World Conference on Church, Community and State, July 12–26, 1937.

5. Finally, that the Conference delegates stated that they were issuing a call to all the churches in the world to intercede for their suffering brethren in Germany.[19]

Melle and Schmidt remained silent throughout the debate but the following day they submitted a strenuous objection. Two days after, when the delegates denounced the suppression of minorities, Melle addressed the conference. In his speech he stated:

> "We have looked upon the national rule of the German people as a deed of divine providence . . . .we have joined our gratitude that God in his providence has sent a leader who was able to banish the danger of Bolshevism in Germany and to rescue a nation of from sixty to seventy millions from the abyss of despair to which it had been led through the world war and the Treaty of Versailles and its wretched consequences, and to give this nation a new faith in its mission and future. I wish to God that that the churches had not failed so utterly in the times past, and that God might have used them to render a similar service to our nation."[20]

The time lapse meant that this was a well-crafted speech, not an unthinking reaction to what had been said by the conference delegates. Melle could not argue that he did not fully own what he had said: that Hitler was divinely appointed, that there was a divine purpose to what was taking place in Germany, and that he wished this had happened earlier. Bishop George Bell, who had led the group that had written the statement that so offended Melle and Schmidt, claimed that the delay in the response was because Melle and Schmidt had received instructions from the German Embassy in London to act.[21] Even if this were true, and it would certainly confirm that Melle was in the pocket of the Nazi regime, he could not avoid the fact that his response came in the shadow of the book burnings,[22] the

---

19. Neely, "Oxford 1937: Are They Right?"

20. Statement by the Right Reverend Bishop Otto Melle of Berlin at the World Church Conference in Oxford on July 22, 1937. Anglo German Information Service, London. Document held in the Imperial War Museum Archives, London.

21. Neely., "Oxford 1937: Are They Right?"

22. The ritual burning of any books in 1933 that were deemed to be a cultural challenge to the Nazis.

night of the long knives,[23] the Nuremburg Laws,[24] the detention of political opponents without trial, and the establishment of concentration camps. As late as 1938 Melle[25] believed that history would "detect God's leading finger" at work.

A further tour of the United States in 1939 cemented the view that Melle was a firm believer in the Nazi regime. His leadership encouraged other Methodists to support the regime: ministers, students and lay people became members of the Party, and the church boasted of their membership. Methodist journals promoted Nazi publications and ministers encouraged congregants to support Hitler.[26] In order to understand this level of support it has been argued that because Methodism was seen as a "foreign sect" in that it was not part of the state-recognized church, its origins were British, and it was part of the United Methodist Church of the United States, its members had to prove their loyalty more than those from the more indigenous denominations. Whether that is sufficient to explain the actions of what was effectively one of the most loyal Christian churches to the Nazi regime is difficult to judge. What we do know is that when a church in Schneidemühl wrote to Hitler for a donation towards a new organ, Hitler responded with a personal cheque to the sum of ten thousand Reichsmarks, and that Hitler was godfather to Methodist twins and to a minister's son.[27] After the war when evidence of the Nazi atrocities became more widely known, Melle and his supporters would argue that his was the only course of action he could take to preserve the Methodist Church intact. That would be more verifiable had some resistance amongst Methodists come to light, but to date there appears to be no record of such, sadly. In his analysis of the situation Blaich concluded that the Methodist Church, alongside his own Adventist movement and the Baptists, were led by people inadequate to the task.[28]

This whole area of the churches in Nazi Germany is a mammoth topic and no single chapter can do it justice. We could have explored how the

---

23. The assassination of many of Hitler's leading political opponents in 1934 that consolidated his hold on power.

24. These included the legislation that deemed anyone a Jew with just one grandparent who was Jewish.

25. Blaich, "A Tale of Two Leaders," 215.

26. Blaich, "A Tale of Two Leaders," 215.

27. Blaich, "A Tale of Two Leaders," 217.

28. Blaich, "A Church in Crisis."

Nazis sought to create a new church known as the German Christians. We could have explored a comparison between Protestant and Roman Catholic responses; the claim that Roman Catholics on the ground were more likely than their Protestant counterparts to engage in the rescue of Jews could be down to the fact that they were more international in their vision, looking to Rome rather than the state. We could have explored why it was that Pope Pius XII withheld his predecessor's encyclical that denounced the Nazis. But neither time nor space allows us to do so. We have merely scratched the surface of the complexities and the moral dilemmas facing Bonhoeffer and Melle.

What we can do now is merely review a comment on the view that resistance as a consequence of theological argument was limited and pretty well ineffective against the tide of popular opinion. Anyone who offered some form of criticism was quickly rounded upon, not only by the state but by the people. Paul Tillich would contrast the cross with the swastika, a "crooked cross;" Gotthilf Schenkel would compare the self-assertion of Hitler with the humility and compassion of Christ, finding the greeting "Heil Hitler" particularly blasphemous. Ina Gschlössl, a pastor in Cologne, would argue that despite the separation of church and state Christians were called to attend to the spiritual realm first and foremost, getting oneself right before God before addressing the state. One of the few writers to speak out against attacks on Jews was Lilly Farnke. She lamented the inaction of churches and called upon them to rise in defence of Jews.[29] But none of this was enough. The greatest crime in the history of the human race, and indeed in the Christian church, was about to take place.

It had been a gift to the Nazis that they would come to power on the 450th anniversary of Luther's birth. They made great capital out of it. Nothing gave the Nazis more credibility for their actions than seconding Luther to their ranks. It was no coincidence that his document "The Jews and Their Lies," referred to earlier, should go through many reprints in that time. Luther's blueprint for the Holocaust was about to be realised. Celebrations were held across Europe for the anniversary and Hitler was seen to be the new Luther, challenging the old order and ushering in a whole new age.[30] Many Nazi leaders, even those without Christian convictions, would embrace Jesus as one of their own as he too had struggled against the Jews.[31]

---

29. Plant, *How Theologians Decide*, 152.
30. Steigmann-Gall, *The Holy Reich*, 1.
31. Steigmann-Gall, *The Holy Reich*, 266.

We cannot escape the fact that many Nazis were Christians; many pastors joined the Nazi Party, Martin Niemöller's brother Wilhelm amongst them (in 1923).[32] Goebbels remained a nominal Catholic and Hitler never actually renounced his baptism into the Catholic Church. Historian of the period Ian Kershaw wrote: "The latent *antisemitism* and apathy of the German people sufficed to allow the increasingly criminal 'dynamic' hatred of the Nazi regime the autonomy it needed to set in motion the Holocaust."[33] It remains true that the German people were in the main baptised Christians.

The enormity of the Holocaust is overwhelming; the fact that it happened in the heart of Christian Europe and was conducted by many who attended church on a Sunday is deeply distressing. How can we ever come to terms with it? The truth is we can't. Nothing could make amends for what has been done in the name of Christ: the persecution of Jews over two millennia reached its abhorrent zenith with the use of Zyklon B in the gas chambers of Auschwitz. Nothing can be compared with it; the sheer hatred that was channeled in a calculating fashion into the Final Solution was unprecedented. Yet somehow it was nothing new. Jews had been herded into ghettoes before, they had been forced to wear identifiable clothing and yellow badges, they had been stripped of their dignity, removed from office, bankrupted, robbed, even massacred. The only difference was that in the industrialised world the methods had become so much more effective. The great fear now is that, as the industrial age gives way to the digital communications age, the prejudice can reach new levels both in terms of rapidity and impact.

What also happened under the Nazis was the shift in what was acceptable. Many people behaved in ways that under normal circumstance they would have spurned. The boundaries moved, step by step the hatred deepened, and the actions grew. Once their previously respected neighbor was dehumanized and removed from sight, it became that much easier to support laying waste an entire people and culture. The personal and the individual was lost in the mass.

On one visit to Auschwitz in the room where mounds of clothing are held I was captivated by a floral print dress. The star and number were still attached. After I left I reflected on this one item of clothing and the words flowed from me.

32. Ericksen, *Complicity in the Holocaust*, 186.
33. Fischer, *The History of an Obsession*, 403.

Edging Closer to Catastrophe

What color You brought to life:
You, whom I cannot name and will not number;
yet numbered by those who claimed Your name
and believed in colors just two, testaments old and new;
black and white their view, and turned black to blue, your flesh tones too.
Battered, beaten and bruised, now frail and tender form,
that which was once so proudly hailed and held,
in Father's arms and Mother's shawl.

What color You brought to life:
dressed in floral print
and in newborn dawn daylight glint.
What sin could You commit in minds of evil intent,
You, the Voice, in place and time,
silenced, transported and transformed,
without bread and wine?

What color You brought to life:
through ritual, festival and feast,
tradition and Torah, Seder and Hanukah;
Your vibrancy and vitality
toned down for safety and security;
But through purposeful prejudice,
arrogance and hostility
You were led away, dragged away,
toward no "Good" Friday.

What color You brought to life:
to those who knew you, "one in a million,"
but, to those who didn't, one in six,
"a statistic" claimed dictator's creed,
just a number in a log he reads.

What color You brought to life:
You who, with all, lost all, but hand-sewn yellow star;
With others you were brought from near and far.
For hope and life you craved,
You who gave

and from whom was taken, long-held dreams through *shtetl's* devastation.
You who loved and lived in flesh and blood
To lose and die in Auschwitz mud.

Chapter 8

"Of Course This Isn't *Antisemitism*"

IN ENGLAND A LARGE section of fans in a soccer crowd hiss. Why? Because their team are playing Spurs, the club with the highest number of Jewish supporters in the Premier League, and their hissing symbolizes the sound of gas. A car races through a Jewish community in north Manchester and its occupants scream out of the window: "Hitler was right." Protesters on the streets of capital cities across Europe hold up placards that portray a kind of algebra: a Star of David equals a swastika. A website gives advice on how far you can go to abuse Jewish members of the British Parliament without falling foul of the law. And so it goes on.

My good friend Eva Schloss is the posthumous stepsister of Anne Frank because her mother, Elfriede, survived the Holocaust and Elfriede married Anne's father Otto. Eva said to me in August 2014 that she felt that the hatred was the worst since the war. Having herself survived Auschwitz, Eva has never been one to exaggerate. Since then the recorded number of anti-Semitic attacks has increased significantly. *Antisemitism* is back with an increasing vengeance across Europe from Poland and Hungary to Paris and London.

What would the liberators of Belsen and Buchenwald have made of it? Those liberators who I have personally met over the course of my ministry were understandably horrified that anyone or any regime could have done what the Nazis and their collaborators did to Jews in the Holocaust. They were very much aware of the steps that led to the camps: graffiti, broken windows, desecration of gravestones, boycotts, book burnings, exaggeration, and lies.

But the opening decades of the twenty-first century have witnessed an extraordinary and deepening level of contempt toward Jews. In recent years it has become acceptable, even laudable in some quarters, to express anti-Jewish sentiment. The margins of decency have shifted; the checks that were once in place seem to have been dismissed as no longer relevant. And those who dared question such hostility have been ridiculed or even seen as some kind of social deviant; nowhere more so than in the Christian church. Has the church and her members not learnt from history? Do they not appreciate how theology and practice over the centuries have echoes in the present? Are they not aware of the links? Can they not see that they are being played by Israel's enemies every bit as much as Hitler played the church in 1930s Germany? Have they read history at all? The answer to each of these questions appears to be a frustratingly tragic no.

Centuries of Judeophobia seem to have hardwired many Christians to be nervous of Jews and even suspicious of their motives. Those who verbally attack Israel, the only Jewish state in the world, without a decent knowledge and understanding of Judeophobia in the history of the church seem unable to hear the echoes of that past in their hostility: from the misplaced belief that Jews killed the Christ to the claim that Israel is hostile to religions other than Judaism; from the medieval myth that Jews poisoned wells to the claim that Israel tampers with the water supply to Palestinians; from the vile allegation that Jews sacrificed Christian children to drink their blood at Passover to the claim that Israeli forces shoot to wound Palestinians so that later in hospital their organs may be transferred to wealthy Jews; from the hostility toward enforced usury to the claim that Jewish bankers control today's money markets; from the Protocols of Zion to the claim that a Jewish syndicate conspires to create social unrest through the media; from the boycott of Jewish businesses in 1930s Germany to pro-Palestinian demonstrations outside shops in the UK; from book burnings in Munich to the trolling on social media of musicians who play in Tel Aviv; from supporting Nazis to doing the PR for Hamas and Hezbollah; from Luther's "The Jews and Their Lies" to one of the most invidious documents for a very long time: the so-called "Open Letter." This was produced by a number of Christian organizations in Palestine in June 2017.[1] It claims that Israel was founded on a twisted theological premise, thereby debunking the Old Testament prophets and the Jewish understanding of covenant; it even calls

---

1. Open letter from the National Coalition of Christian Organizations in Palestine (NCCOP) to the World Council of Churches, June 2017.

"Of Course This Isn't Antisemitism"

for Christians to withdraw from dialogue with Jews and for churches to take legal action against Christian organizations that "discredit" their work.

Judeophobia is more than just an irrational fear; we have seen from the previous chapters that it has a habit of turning nastier still. All of the examples at the beginning of this chapter are but a few steps from contempt to eliminationism, i.e. the destruction of Jewry, in this case the only Jewish state in the world: Israel.

Eliminating the state of Israel is the end goal of many across the Middle East. Under Yasser Arafat's watch this was the stated aim of the Palestinian Liberation Organization and later Fatah. At Camp David, Israel made the extraordinary offer to withdraw from 95 percent of the West Bank and even that was not acceptable to Arafat.

As we have seen, eliminationism has often been at the very heart of much Christian belief over the centuries. There still persists the view that Jews are no longer instruments of God's will, their religion having been superseded by the church. As such their continuing presence is a curious anomaly to many Christians. On many occasions I have heard variations of: "but surely their religion is now obsolete!" If anything the Holocaust should have rendered the hatred of Jews obsolete, but unfortunately that was not the case. Very soon after they were liberated many survivors from the camps found that little had changed. On returning to their former homes to take up residence again, many discovered that their properties had been occupied since they were forced from them and the new occupants were not willing to move out. Hostility toward the returning Jews was not uncommon; indeed, the age-old blood libel was still circulating in some countries and in July 1946 a number of Jews were killed in Kielce by Poles who falsely claimed that Jews had kidnapped a Christian boy and murdered a number of others.[2]

If anyone at the gates of a newly-liberated concentration camp thought that *antisemitism* was now so discredited that it could never be repeated, they would have to think again. Writing in 2002, the leader of the German Jewish community, Paul Spiegel, commented on the resurgence of *antisemitism*:

> "If anyone had told me in 1945 that in Germany Jewish cemeteries would again be desecrated, synagogues set afire, foreigners hounded, I would have declared him to be mad. Shortly after the war the philosophers Horkheimer and Adorno wrote in their book 'The

2. Goldhagen, *The Devil that Never Dies*, 118.

Dialectics of the Enlightenment: after Auschwitz' *antisemitism* is no longer possible. At this, today, we are tempted to burst out laughing, bitterly . . . I experience here very much *antisemitism* and very much xenophobia."[3]

Even the dead were not allowed to rest. In his book *Golden Harvest* Jan Tomasz Gross draws on a photograph taken immediately after the Second World War. It is of Polish peasants standing together at the end of a hard day's work. As Gross states, it could easily be taken for any central European workforce gathering in their harvest, except their harvest is somewhat unusual. In front of the laborers are human bones including skulls. They are standing on top of a mound of ashes, the ashes of 800,000 Jews cremated at Treblinka between July 1942 and October 1943. The men and women have been sifting through the ashes, and those human remains that the heat of the crematoria didn't quite destroy, in search of any gold or jewels that the Nazis may have overlooked.[4]

Research in Germany in 1952 found that 37 percent of the population still believed that there were too many Jews in the country;[5] which is extraordinary bearing in mind that 160,000 German Jews had been killed in the Holocaust just a few years earlier. By 1987 research concluded that 13 percent still felt that there were too many Jews in Germany and that they should migrate to Israel. It is an interesting comparison to consider the graffiti of 1930s Europe with that of twenty-first century Europe. In the 1930s the message was "Jews go to Palestine;" today it is more likely to be "Jews out of Palestine."

The scale and impact of the Holocaust was so enormous that since then all forms of Judeophobia other than violent *antisemitism* are viewed by many as insignificant. Many see no harm in a sermon that ignores the context of the gospel accounts and fails to address the anti-Judaism of the writer. Even during the 500th anniversary in 2017 of the Reformation, few bothered to consider Luther's diatribe against the Jews. As for singing hymns that happen to refer to the Jews as being a spiritually blind, lost race, who really cares?

Herein lies the danger. As we have already seen, Judeophobia has a pernicious habit of changing according to the times. Anti-Judaism hasn't gone away, nor has *antisemitism*, but a new form of Judeophobia, fed by

---

3. Goldhagen, *The Devil that Never Dies*, 108.
4. Gross, *Golden Harvest*.
5. Goldhagen, *The Devil that Never Dies*, 121.

"Of Course This Isn't Antisemitism"

both earlier forms, has emerged. It has become possible for those that promote it to claim that they are neither anti-Jewish (religiously prejudiced) nor anti-Semitic (racially prejudiced) because they are solely motivated by their desire for peace in the Middle East and justice for the Palestinians. The fact that they are campaigning against the only Jewish state in the world seems to pass them by. The fact that Israel is the safest place in the region for Christians, other religious minorities, and members of the LGBTQI community is totally ignored. The fact that Israel is the only functioning liberal democracy amidst autocratic regimes is immaterial. Chaos and utter destruction can reign in neighboring countries, chemical weapons used, millions forced from their homes, women sold in sex-slave markets, Christians, Jews and other religious minorities be virtually non-existent in those countries, and Muslims be massacred in their tens of thousands by those who claim to be Muslim, but all this is outside the sphere of the "pro-Palestinian" campaign. It is deemed far more important for them to lobby church conferences, unions, universities, and local authorities over 0.25 percent of the region than be troubled by what is going on in the other 99.75 percent.

Any focus there may have been on the tackling of continuing religious and racial prejudice has tended to overlook the fact that a new form of Judeophobia, in the guise of political action termed anti-Zionist or pro-Palestinian, has gained a strong foothold in almost every section of British society. To treat this new expression of hatred with any degree of complacency is highly dangerous. It was complacency built on centuries of deep-seated contempt that led to the catastrophe that was the Holocaust. I fear that a similar catastrophe is just around the corner. At a Seder (Passover meal) in 2018, just as we got to the point in the meal when the ten plagues are recounted, the acting rabbi asked those around the table if he was alone in thinking that they had enjoyed a few decades of tolerance and relative peace but that now "the situation" was getting bleak again. There was a silence in the room. Next to me sat a man whose extended family had perished in Lithuania. Opposite me was a man whose mother was the sole survivor of her family in Ukraine. Further along was a man whose father had been rescued by Nicholas Winton's valiant efforts at saving Czech children through the kinderstransport program (no other family member survived). Eventually the silence was broken by a woman who said "it could never happen again." No, *it* couldn't, not in the same way as before. But *it* could happen in another form and maybe just as catastrophic, if not more so. From what we have learnt from our brief overview of two thousand years is that once it has found a place in which it can flourish, Judeophobia tends to be pretty unstoppable. When the church was strong and influential, the hatred was justified by its theology; when reason rather than religion became central to western thought, it was cultural prejudice that led Jews to not being treated on equal terms. When this became unacceptable and difficult to maintain as Jews assimilated, race became the foundation of the hatred that led to the Holocaust. Today, post-Auschwitz, more than seventy years after the gas chambers and crematoria were destroyed, the shadow of *antisemitism* and its horrendous result still holds some moral restraint. It is not uncommon to hear someone claim that they are not racist or anti-Semitic yet espouse the vilest views, hold irrational hatred for, and maintain disproportionate criticism of Israel and its people. This has led to the grip that held some back from Judeophobia loosening year by year. What has been unleashed in recent years could be just as destructive as the Holocaust. Meanwhile there is little criticism in Europe of Iran and her allies threatening to eradicate Jews from the Middle East.

It is claimed, not without some justification, that events in the Middle East since the founding of the state of Israel in 1948 determine the level of Judeophobia in the West. The relationship between Israel and her neighbors is paramount in any understanding of prejudice against Jews over the last half-century or so. Between the Suez Crisis of 1956 and the Yom Kippur War of 1973 a great sea change took place in European, especially British, attitudes toward the state of Israel. There was without doubt a degree of hostility all along, not least because of the impossible position British military personnel in the British Mandate found themselves in, post-Second World War. Seen to be an army of occupation by both Jews and Arabs alike, the British were caught between a rock and a hard place. Both sides had national aspirations: the Zionists, those wanting to create a safe home for Jews, had great reason to question British intentions as the latter sought to prevent survivors from the concentration camps from entering the country; the Arabs wanted the whole of the area covered by the Mandate for themselves. In the British press, imagery from recent years was deployed to attack the armed revolt by Jews. Jews were accused of believing themselves to be a "master race." The Zionists were, again like the Nazis that had sought to eradicate them, seeking "living space."[6] Equating the actions of Zionists, and later Israel as a whole, with the actions of their Nazi persecutors

---

6. Wistrich, *A Lethal Obsession*, 378.

would become a familiar ploy in the decades to come, as noted at the very beginning of this chapter, where the Star of David is seen to be a version of the swastika.

Arab nationalism was seen as organic and aspirational, whereas Zionism was a colonial movement. Jews were seen as occupiers, even those whose ancestors had been born, lived, and died in the land. The situation has proven to be irresolvable and readers will be well aware of some aspects of the conflict, even if they only come to it from a single narrative, either the Israeli perspective or the Palestinian perspective. Nevertheless, it is necessary for us to consider how this ongoing and tragic conflict has impacted relations between Jews and the rest of the world, in particular the Christian church.

In 1948, five Arab armies massed to crush the fledgling state of Israel and throw the Jews back into the Mediterranean. They failed. Israel was seen by many in the West as a plucky little nation and its founding seemed to be wholly justified. Arab anger did not dissipate. In 1956 when President Nasser of Egypt launched his illegal military action in the Sinai Desert, the Straits of Tiran, and the strategically important Suez Canal, Britain was prepared to side with Israel. But by the time of the Yom Kippur War of 1973, when Arab armies again launched a surprise offensive and very nearly succeeded in their aim of wiping out Israel, Britain was taking a very different approach. In between 1956 and 1973, the Six-Day War of 1967 had changed the mindset. Despite the fact that Israel had again faced utter destruction at the hands of her neighbors, with only a preemptive attack on Arab airfields saving her, the claim made by European powers to be playing an even hand was not entirely accurate. For example, France, not having come to terms with her own complicity in Nazi atrocities during the war, continued to harbor *antisemitism* in the political right and anti-Israel sentiments in the far left. France continued to train Arab pilots for future conflicts with Israel. As well as training Arab pilots, Britain withheld arms bound for Israel that had already been paid for.

The conquest and occupation in 1967 of Jordanian land to the west of the river Jordan up to and including east Jerusalem (seized incidentally by the Jordanians in 1948), and of course the taking of Gaza from the Egyptians and the Golan Heights from the Syrians, has remained the main source of contention ever since. The holy site known by Muslims as the Noble Sanctuary (Harem esh-Sharif) or by Jews as the Temple Mount also fell into Israeli hands. It is often overlooked that Israel almost immediately handed custody of the site back to Jordan and it has remained under the Waqf guardianship ever since. It is the most contested plot of land in the world: the site of Abraham's would-be sacrifice of Isaac, the Jewish temple and holy of holies, the place where Muhammad is said to have been lifted into heaven, and for Christians, a place where Jesus visited during the festivals.

It is not possible for us to properly explore the full details of the ongoing Israeli-Palestinian conflict and it is not the intention of this chapter to do so; we merely have to know the briefest of timelines to appreciate the most recent expression of Judeophobia in the West.

In his monumental book *A Lethal Obsession*, the late historian Robert Wistrich identifies the 1982 Lebanon War as a significant moment in the increasing hatred in Britain toward Israel. He cites numerous examples of media reports where Lebanese and Palestinian casualties were grossly exaggerated and which drew on misplaced Holocaust imagery. In that year more than fifty university campuses were targeted in an anti-Israel campaign and the following year trade unions passed resolutions calling on a boycott of Israel. Much of this campaign was initiated by the far left and so many, including those within the Christian church, have swallowed Trotskyite mantras such as: "resolve the Israel-Palestine conflict and there will be peace in the Middle East." This is merely a version of a statement from the Socialist Worker Party in 1982: "There will be no peace in the Middle East while the State of Israel continues to exist."[7] It was as if the far left and far right were in competition with one another to see which could be the most vociferous in their hatred of Israel. There were claims that Israel would turn Beirut into a *"gas chamber by using chemical weapons"* and that there were *"concentration camps"* filled with Lebanese and Palestinians. It was also alleged that the British Prime Minister of the day, Margaret Thatcher, was failing to rein in the Israelis because of a "Zionist Plot" led by her Jewish cabinet colleagues and the newly appointed head of the BBC, Stuart Young.[8] Interestingly, British Labor Member of Parliament Tam Dalyell would make similar claims of Tony Blair twenty years later in May 2003 over the Iraq War.[9] Wistrich also claims that there has been a certain degree of reluctance on the part of the BBC to use the term "terror" to describe atrocities carried out by Palestinians, preferring instead to describe

---

7. Wistrich, *A Lethal Obsession*, 382.
8. Wistrich, *A Lethal Obsession*, 383.
9. Wistrich, *A Lethal Obsession*, 385.

the terrorists as "militants" or "radicals."[10] If this is so then it doesn't take long to come to the conclusion that the drip, drip, drip of biased reporting could well have influenced public opinion with regards to Israel and the Jews over the decades.

Even from this very brief snapshot of the decades after the defeat of the Nazi regime, we can begin to see that similar characteristics are to be found in the age-old anti-Judaism of the church, the *antisemitism* that led to Auschwitz, and the anti-Zionism of today.

What makes the Judeophobia of today so dangerous is that it is political and political ideologies are calls for action; they are not just theories on how the world is.[11] Anti-Zionism has the potential to be as dangerous as the anti-Judaism of the medieval Church and even, indeed, the *antisemitism* of the Nazis. It also has the added "bonus" of allowing its protagonists the luxury of claiming that they are not anti-Semitic because their views (prejudice) are not based on race, nor even religion. Their claim is helped by the fact that many Jews tend to be more identified by their country of origin (Britain, France, etc.) than perhaps ever before and less aligned with Jews from elsewhere.[12] The one thing that binds them together, according to their detractors, is the state of Israel and are all, therefore, "legitimate" targets in the campaign to "free" the Palestinians.

One early commentator on how centuries of Judeophobia had led to the gas chambers and is now becoming more political was American Methodist minister and academic Franklin Littell (1917–2009). He was well-qualified to do so. He attended a Nuremburg rally in 1939 and was ejected by a stormtrooper because of his protestations. After the war Littell spent ten years in Germany as Chief Protestant Religious Adviser in the high command. In his role he was part of the denazification program and interviewed many Nazis who also happened to be Christian. Littell was under no illusions about the rise of anti-Zionism:

> "The new code word for *Antisemitism* is Anti-Zionism, whether the slogan be uttered by Communists, Arab League propagandists, adherents of the "New Left," or liberal Protestants. . . . No one can be an enemy of Zionism and be a friend of Jewish people

---

10. Wistrich, *A Lethal Obsession*, 386.
11. Goldhagen, *The Devil that Never Dies*, 36.
12. Goldhagen, *The Devil that Never Dies*, 17.

today—not the czar, not the Soviets, not the Deutsche Christen, not the United Church observer."[13]

In challenging the rise of this new expression of Judeophobia, Littell also argued that "Ziondom" (his term) has greater claim to scriptural foundation than Christendom.[14]

The politically-motivated anti-Zionism of recent decades has partly come about as a consequence of the church losing yet more of its influence, as well as from a degree of moral restraint imposed by the Holocaust (in other words the shame at the outcome of religious and racial prejudice), and a public less inclined to tolerate such prejudice. There are now far fewer people than once was the case who are prepared to hear and react to a church that still has issues over who killed the Christ or whether the church has superseded Judaism. But the seed sown by the church over two millennia continue to bear fruit. Indeed because of the fertile ground in which Judeophobia existed and flourished for so long it is no surprise that anti-Zionism is now present and highly visible in much of what remains of today's Christian church. For the church, having failed to convince the world of the need to eliminate Jews through theology and the failure of the Nazis to do so through the Final Solution (though not for want of trying by either party), the weapon of choice is now political. After all, the political and theological can be easily interwoven because every act of love is a political expression. But, as we should know by now, being divorced from the state allowed the Nazis a free hand, or in other words to act without any moral constraints.

The two kingdoms doctrine had been shown up for what it was, a deeply flawed belief that enabled the German churches to fail spectacularly in the moment of their greatest challenge. The newly-emerging liberation theologies of the 1970s drove home the need for the church to be more

---

13. Littell, *The Crucifixion of the Jews*, 97.

14. Littell, *The Crucifixion of the Jews*, 95. John Grauel was a contemporary of Franklin Littell. Born in 1917, he too became a Methodist Minister. In late 1944 or early 1945 he heard that 700,000 Jews had been killed by the Nazis and their accomplices (he thought that if someone had have suggested the figure was nearer six million he would have thought them demented). He committed himself to the relief of Jews and later travelled aboard the *Exodus*, the ship from Europe to Haifa, with Holocaust survivors. He pressed the newly-established United Nations to recognize the state of Israel and would go on to be amongst the very first to lead Jewish teenagers on tours of the concentration camps. The Israeli Prime Minister Gold Meir would later recognize his contribution to the establishing of the State of Israel and he received a number of awards for his work. He died at home in New Jersey in 1986 and was buried in Jerusalem with full Israeli Naval honors.

active in the political realm. As a consequence, the church became even more active in protecting the weak against the strong, in supporting those seeking liberation from the oppressor, and in standing beside those fighting for justice. This, of course, is an honorable and undeniable feature of Christian social action but in many Christian minds there's no clearer example of the weak, oppressed and unjustly treated than Palestinians suffering at the hands of the "all-powerful, highly-connected, fabulously-resourced Israeli (Jewish) aggressor." The only problem with this mindset is that it lacks a comprehensive perspective and fails to stand up to rigorous socio-political and historical scrutiny.

The near-complete failure of the Christian church to address the Judeophobia of the gospel accounts and its teaching and practice over the centuries has left generation after generation of Christian ministers ignorant of their collusion, albeit in most cases innocent collusion, of contempt against the Jews. Many will attend meetings and rallies, hear a not entirely-balanced view of the situation in Israel-Palestine, stand at conference podia, preach from pulpits, and repeat the rhetoric of the past without even realizing it. Centuries of uncorrected contempt cannot help but influence the perception many Christians have of Jews, even for those who occasionally seek to guard what they say in public. Nor can it help but impact Jews who will surely hear more clearly than any other the same old prejudice from their Christian neighbors, now reformed into something seemingly new. There is little doubt that unchecked Judeophobia within the Christian church, influenced by political theologies and the vile propaganda of the European far left, together with a growing awareness of Arab and Islamic hostility toward Jews and their national aspirations, have led to an obsessive campaign against the only Jewish state in the world. It was once the case that Jews were herded into certain areas and later ghettos to ensure control. They thus became an easy target whenever a scapegoat was required, be it a when the holy sites were being conquered, the outbreak of the Black Death, or economic downturn. Today the target is just as easily identified and located: Israel.

As mentioned above, there seem to be blind spots for many anti-Zionists; these include a wider perspective and a more sophisticated historical analysis of the socio-political landscape in the Middle East. Gaza and the West Bank have become rallying points for Judeophobes. Readily overlooking the frequent attempts by her neighbors to eliminate the legitimate state of Israel, the anti-Zionists also fail to properly address the despairingly horrific violence elsewhere in the region. It all begins by not being willing to admit that there never was a Palestinian State. Prior to the British liberation of the land in 1917 the area was occupied for four hundred years by the Ottomans. After 1948 the West Bank was part of Jordan. As a consequence of the Six-Day War of 1967, the Jordanian border was pushed back to the Jordan River when Israel took control. Many of its citizens were "left behind," others fled, as did Jews to Israel from neighboring countries, as Jews had twenty years earlier in 1948, though few anti-Zionists are reluctant to sufficiently admit such facts. It is sometimes claimed that the main exodus of Jews to Israel were those fleeing Europe from the early twentieth-century pogroms through to the aftermath of the Holocaust; what is readily ignored by so many anti-Zionists is that around 850,000 Jews had to flee Arab countries between 1948 and the early 1970s, 260,000 of them between 1948 and 1951 alone, which accounted for 56 percent of the immigrant population of Israel.[15] The anti-Zionist claim that Palestinians were "ethnically cleansed" from the land is as one-sided as it gets: Jews were also forced from their ancient homes, well-established businesses, and countries they had called "home" for centuries and in some cases millennia. Jews are hardly present in any Arab country today, yet one and a half million Arabs in Israel continue to enjoy the protection of the state. The concern that the pro-Palestinian lobby has for those Palestinians in the West Bank and Gaza that have unquestionably suffered is noble and just, but when that concern is as narrowly focused as it is, leading to anti-Israeli sentiments and actions, then it crosses a line. Where is the equivalent concern for the plight of others who missed out in the post-First World War settlement and re-drawing of borders? Take, for example, the Kurds. Fourteen to twenty million found themselves oppressed by Turkey alone,[16] which is more than twice the population of Israel and between three and five times the population of the West Bank and Gaza. Then there are concerns about the relationship Palestinians have had with their "host countries." That relationship has been turbulent to say the least. In Jordan in 1970 they sought to overthrow King Hussein which led to much bloodshed. In the 1970s the Palestinians made an attempt to take over Lebanon and precipitated a devastating civil war. Their leader Yasser Arafat (1929–2004) was an Egyptian born in Cairo and through his Palestinian Liberation Organization (PLO) turned terrorism

---

15. Shindler, *A History of Modern Israel*, 63–64.
16. Goldhagen, *The Devil that Never Dies*, 159.

into a global phenomenon.[17] So Israel is not alone in having a problem with Palestinians, but Palestinian supporters and anti-Zionists in the Christian churches seem blind to many of the facts.

It is extraordinary that some Palestinian children are taught to glorify martyrdom and to honor suicide bombers. Why aren't members of the Christian churches, rightly keen to implement child protection policies within their own denominations, unable to criticize the appalling abuse of children in the Palestinian communities? Wistrich notes that maps in many Palestinian school textbooks do not even refer to "Israel" and the existence 5.3 million Jews in the land.[18] Many who support the Palestinian cause claim that Jews are bent on creating an Israeli "Super State" stretching from the Nile to the Euphrates; this would be laughable if it were not so invidious.[19]

This wholly disproportionate focus within the churches on Israel-Palestine is unhelpful in the extreme. It is adding to the drip, drip, drip of anti-Zionist rhetoric from the far left and playing on a deep subconscious Judeophobia embedded through Christian theology and practice over millennia. One clear example of this was how the Judeophobes leapt on the centenary of the Balfour Declaration of 1917. The Balfour Declaration was a letter from the British Foreign Secretary Arthur Balfour to Lord Walter Rothschild which was to be passed on to the Zionist Federation:

> His Majesty's government view with favor the establishment in Palestine of a national home for the Jewish people, and will use their best endeavors to facilitate the achievement of this object, it being clearly understood that nothing shall be done which may prejudice the civil and religious rights of existing non-Jewish communities in Palestine, or the rights and political status enjoyed by Jews in any other country.

On the centenary of the declaration, the pro-Palestinian/anti-Zionist groups sought to blame most of the suffering of the Palestinians post-1948 on this letter, overlooking all the other treaties and agreements of the First and early post-First World War years that affected many more millions elsewhere in the Middle East as well as Africa, Europe, and especially the Balkans. There was also a failure on their part to admit that the land had been occupied and turbulent for centuries prior to 1917. Many factors

---

17. Goldhagen, *The Devil that Never Dies*, 161.
18. Wistrich, *A Lethal Obsession*, 726.
19. Wistrich, *A Lethal Obsession*, 722.

other than the Balfour Declaration conspired to make the conflict between Israelis and Palestinians seemingly irresolvable, not least the Sykes-Picot agreement of 1916 that began the drawing up of the borders right across the Middle East, of which Israel is but 0.25 percent.

It is clear that the anti-Zionists have found a willing home in many Christian churches. For many members of a religion that has spent two thousand years both denigrating the root from which it grew and claiming that the death of Jesus was the reason why Jews did not have a homeland to call their own, the return of Jews to form the state of Israel has been anathema. Whilst the more evangelical and fundamentalist wings of the Christian church, holding firmly to biblical prophecy, have embraced the founding of the state of Israel as a sign of divine purpose, the tensions between conservatism and liberalism within the church has found in Israel a supreme stick to beat each other with, even when they don't recognize it themselves: if it's not debates on sex that sets the church pulse racing, then it's Israel.

A further difficulty is that many in the church fail to recognize that radical Islam no longer has an equivalent in Christianity. We find it difficult to imagine that a religion, albeit in an increasingly extreme form, seeks to take over a state and govern the country using a rigid interpretation of Scripture. In the Christian world this has not been so since the decades after the Reformation, which is why the anti-Zionists in the church underestimate the threat to Israel posed by her neighbors. Those Christians who campaign against Israel are not always working to the same rules as many of their Muslim counterparts in the Middle East, and the aims tend to be wholly different. Whilst liberation from oppression is the goal of some, the elimination of Israel, meaning of course Jews, from the region is the goal of many. I fear that some in the church are unwilling to admit this. Others, I would hope unintentionally, are just unable to grasp it. Innocent ignorance is perhaps the only way that I can find some sense of relief in my ongoing frustration with my sisters and brothers in the church who speak and act so forcefully and so disproportionately against Israel.

As we have already hinted, it could be argued that *antisemitism* was repressed in the early decades after the Second World War, in part due to a realization of where it had led. Not so now, more than seven decades after the last Jews were liberated from the camps and began their lifelong struggle to face living again. Judeophobia is rising and rising fast. "Of course, it isn't *antisemitism*," so many think and claim. But anti-Zionism is a form of Judeophobia as pernicious as any before it. Memories are fading, survivors are dying, the guilt at not having done enough is receding and suddenly it's not just anti-Zionism that is the sole source of Judeophobia in our world; Jews are again being attacked no matter their views on Israel, simply because they are Jews. The same old tropes are being repeated again and again with an increasing frequency that should set alarm bells ringing throughout the thinking world.

It becomes deeply frustrating when attempts at a more rational approach illicit a hostile response. More informed analysis, either historical, religious, or political, when it leads to a contrary view, or even a more nuanced view, is often met with a kind of moral indignation. In a 1938 lecture in Paris, French philosopher Jacques Maritain stated that *antisemitism* falsifies by exaggeration the factual data and removes any hope of mutual understanding and collaboration. This, according to Maritain, is because *antisemitism* is a disease that destroys the state of mind necessary for understanding on both sides: "On the one side directly, and on the other by the passions of protest and resentment which it provokes in response, so that exasperation and misunderstanding, like reciprocal evils, grow irremediably in the minds of both parties."[20]

The incredulity of the anti-Zionist is that there is suffering and there is only one side to blame; it is that plain and simple. The response of the anti-Zionist is just as straightforward: campaign, boycott, divest, and impose sanctions. Those who dare to question whether this is the best way forward for both sides are seen as part of the "great Jewish conspiracy." It is a catch-all argument because those who seek balance are viewed by the anti-Zionists as a great threat to their campaign for justice. The anti-Zionist longs for justice for Palestinians but tends to overlook the need for security and justice for Israeli Jews.

The word "boycott" sends shivers down the spines of Jews, as well it might. We have referred to boycotts of the past and how they led to a further stage of discrimination. There is more than a hint of hypocrisy on the part of many anti-Zionists who campaign for the boycott of Israel. In his book *The Devil Never Dies*, Daniel Goldhagen refers to a survey of academics in the United States who were advocating a boycott of Israel. 627 had signed a petition to the then newly-elected President Obama condemning Israel as an apartheid regime, as racist, as being guilty of ethnocidal atrocities etc. When asked to sign a second letter supporting the oppressed and

---

20. Maritain, *Antisemitism*, 3.

persecuted peoples of other Middle Eastern countries, including women, gays, and lesbians, only 27 of the original 627 did so. Also interesting was the fact that as many as 25 percent of the 627 were associated with faculties that addressed gender and women studies; in other words, they were spending their life's work on rightly raising issues relating to greater gender justice, yet when it came to criticizing Israel a blind eye was being turned to the injustices of her neighbors.[21] In 2017 the British rock group Radiohead faced a huge campaign to discourage them from playing a concert in Tel Aviv. It is extraordinary that one of those urging them to boycott Israel was film director Ken Loach whose film *"I Daniel"* had been shown in Tel Aviv cinemas.

As well as hypocritical campaigns to boycott Israel, another familiar attack is the claim that Jews still control the media; yet even the most cursory glance at the way in which many news outlets cover the Israel-Palestine conflict leaves what was an impartial mind thinking of Israel as the sole aggressor in the region.

As for Holocaust denial I am almost reluctant to even mention it. It seems to me that once it becomes acceptable to deny the Holocaust, or question its magnitude, any false claim is possible; yet the denial persists despite all the evidence, all the witness statements, the survivors' testimonies, the mass graves and documentation. What is especially troubling is the increasing acceptance of Holocaust denial as a legitimate view. Deborah Lipstadt, the American Holocaust historian who was targeted by Holocaust denier David Irving, said that not all opinions are equally valid. How right she was.

In the previous chapter I suggested an amendment to Edmund Burke's famous quote, "In order for evil to flourish, all that is required is for good men to do nothing." Maybe it is indeed equally true that all it takes for evil to flourish is for good people to make the wrong choices. Many did so in 1930s Germany and many are doing so again. Good people have always made wrong choices; it is the cost of having free will. A former Anglican colleague of mine when I served as minister in Manchester, Canon Albert Radcliffe, was the first person to introduce me to the complicity of the church in the path that led to the Holocaust. While speaking alongside another good friend, Rabbi Brian Fox, Albert drew my attention to texts that I had never really recognized before as anti-Jewish. So far as I can recall the presence of anti-Judaism in the gospel accounts in particular

21. Goldhagen, *The Devil that Never Dies*, 41.

was not something that had been mentioned at theological college when I was training for ministry. It was, for me, a moment of enlightenment and helped make so much sense of the verses and passages that I had struggled with up until then. In the years that followed, this newfound knowledge made me read the Christian Scriptures in a wholly new way. I couldn't help but identify those texts that were intentionally anti-Jewish, which brought to mind another error that I can't help but notice each time I see it. As a ten-year-old schoolboy I had been flag monitor at primary school. This meant that on certain saints' days, the Queen's birthday, Battle of Britain Day, VE day and so on, I had to hoist the Union Flag up the school flag pole. For countries with a vertical tricolor, for example, it is an easy task to get it the right way up, but for some it is obvious when it is flying upside down. But the Union Flag of the United Kingdom, like so many, can be flown upside down without many noticing. The broad, not the narrow, white diagonal band of the cross of St. Andrew on the flag has to be at the top, not on the bottom next to the pole. It is a subtle but highly significant difference. Having been flag monitor all those years ago means that I can no longer look at a Union Flag on its pole without checking to see if it is the right way up. Likewise, with anti-Jewish texts in Scripture and indeed *antisemitism* at large in our world, having become aware of their presence elsewhere, I cannot help but clearly identify them in what had been previously unrecognized settings. In some respects, this is a burden, for it has brought me much conflict when I have drawn attention to them, but equally so I believe it is my moral responsibility to address them.

Albert Radcliffe also opened my eyes to a significant dilemma by drawing on an often-overlooked verse attributed to Jesus by Luke: "Therefore consider whether the light in you is not darkness."[22] The text is a warning to us all. How many times have we acted in ways we believed to be right at the time only to later discover that we had got it wrong all along? What must have those German pastors felt when they saw newsreel footage of living skeletons sitting amongst piles of bodies at Belsen? How wrong they had been to support or turn a blind eye to the actions of the Nazi regime. How wrong they had been to uphold the two kingdoms doctrine or continue to blame the Jews for the death of Jesus and for much of society's ills. How wrong they had been to claim that God was pleased to hear the church had superseded Judaism.

22. Luke 11:35.

Here it may be wise to slot in a word of caution. We ought to be wary of those on the side of the Christian spectrum who lobby in support of Israel but whose true motives in doing so are to follow a theology that would seek to convert Jews, or promote the return of the Jews to the land, in order for the Messiah to come again. This too is a form of Judeophobia. It was on an occasion when I had been asked to speak about Israel-Palestine before a conservative Christian audience that in the subsequent discussion some Israel supporters seemed to think it acceptable to claim God had allowed the Holocaust to happen in order for the state of Israel to be founded. So the Christian pro-Zionist lobby can also present many obstacles in the pursuit of peace and reconciliation between the faiths and indeed within the land of Israel-Palestine too. The inherent danger of being pro-one side can lead to being anti-the other; I believe this is not the most productive way forward.

Many will suggest that the Christian church's dialogue with Judaism has come a long way since the darkest episode in our relationship; in some ways this is true, in others it is not. For those readers of this long and sorry history, they will recognize that in some of the things being said and done today there is something of the past. The contempt of the past echoes down the centuries and can still be heard from pulpits, at conference podia, and in church hall meetings. Making common cause with the anti-Zionists outside the church may give some Christians a degree of identity, but history has shown again and again that Judeophobia has a habit of getting out of hand. It doesn't take long for such prejudice to become the prevailing view. Time and again only a catastrophe brought it to a halt. Pray to God that this is not so on this occasion; indeed, may we be brave enough, faithful enough, to do something that few did before us: learn from our history of contempt toward our sisters and brothers and rid ourselves of this vile and pernicious prejudice.

In the novel *The Last of the Just*, the main character is Ernie, a Lamed Vav, one of the legendary thirty-six pious Jews alive at any given point in time; he describes Jesus as a simple Jew, a kind of Hasid, a member of a strictly orthodox Jewish sect; indeed, he was a merciful and gentle man like the Baal Shem Tov, the famous eighteenth-century rabbi who founded Hasidism. Ernie then goes on to suggest to his girlfriend that Jesus and her father would have got on very well because he too was a really good Jew. However, and here comes the twist, Christians may claim they love Jesus but Ernie thinks they may hate him without knowing it. This is because they take up the cross by the wrong end and use it as a sword.[23]

I have met too many people who have been the victims of religious prejudice, including those who managed in part to survive the Holocaust, for me to be silent in the face of Judeophobia today, whatever its form.

Let me conclude with Jan. Jan is the only man with whom I have sat on his own memorial bench. While at Ammerdown Retreat Centre near Bath in England, Jan asked me to join him on a walk round the grounds. As we did so he invited me to sit down on a bench. He asked if I liked the view; I said that I did. He then asked if I liked the bench; I said that I did. "Good," he said, "it is my memorial bench. There is no one left who, when I too have gone, could make sure it is put in the right place. So," he concluded, "I thought I would put it here now, that way I also get to enjoy the view!"

Jan is no longer with us. Many survivors are no longer with us. But my memories of those whom I had the privilege of knowing remain vivid. Their stories have helped form me and my perspectives on this world. Having sat on a memorial bench with Jan, having marveled at Gisela's grace after such adversity, and having never ceased to be impressed by Eva, who seeks to change the world through her extraordinary capacity to participate in speaking tours, what am I to do?

It is for those few that I have had the great privilege of knowing, and to those millions whose stories were never told, that I have dedicated my endeavors in trying to better understand and more effectively combat Judeophobia. I know that as a Christian, there remains a lot I have to learn. There are many people yet to be convinced, and if I want the church to truly love its closest faith neighbor, there is still much for us to do.

---

23. Schwarz-Bart, *The Last of the Just*, 351.

"If there is no God, and these bad things happen anyway, then we have to accept each catastrophe, every evil act, as something 'ordinary'. A meaningless, cruel life. But the existence of a creator, a shining light, instils in us a sense of justice, an ability to balance good and evil, and to recognize that, whatever our differences, our similarities are much stronger because we are all human. And if we look to our parents and our teachers to show us the way towards the light, then we have something to live for."[24]

---

24. Jacobs, *Nine Love Letters*, 212.

Bibliography

Abel, Ernest L. *The Roots of Anti-Semitism*. Cranberry, NJ: Associated University Presses, 1975.

Alderman, Geoffrey. "When the Pogrom of the Valleys Erupted in Wales." https://www.thejc.com/lifestyle/features/when-the-pogrom-of-the-valleys-erupted-in-wales-1.25339

Bale, Anthony. *Feeling Persecuted, Christians, Jews and Images of Violence in the Middle Ages*. London: Reaktion, 2010.

Barrer, Shlomo. *The Doctors of Revolution, 19th-Century Thinkers Who Changed the World*. New York: Thames & Hudson, 2000.

Bendyshe, Thomas. *Anthropological Treatises of Blumenbach and Hunter*. London: Longman, Roberts & Green, 1865.

Blaich, Roland. "A Church in Crisis: Historical Reflections on Leadership." Lecture, Walla Walla University, College Place, WA, May 2015. https://www.wallawalla.edu/about-wwu/marketing-and-university-relations/publications/distinguished-faculty-lectures/roland-blaich/

———. "A Tale of Two Leaders: German Methodists and the Nazi State." *Church History* 70 (2001) 199–225.

Eisenman, Robert. *James the Brother of Jesus*. London: Watkins, 2002.

Elon, Amos. *The Pity of It All: a Portrait of Jews in Germany, 1743–1933*. London: Penguin, 2004.

Erhman, Bart D. "The Gospel of Peter." In *Lost Scriptures*, 31–34. Oxford: Oxford University Press, 2005.

Ericksen, Robert P. *Complicity in the Holocaust: Churches and Universities in Nazi Germany*. Cambridge/New York/Melbourne: Cambridge University Press, 2012.

Felsenstein, Frank. *Anti-Semitic Stereotypes: a Paradigm of Otherness in English Popular Culture 1660–1830*. Baltimore: The John Hopkins University Press, 1995.

Fischer, Klaus P. *The History of an Obsession: German Judeophobia and the Holocaust*. New York: Continuum, 1998.

Florence, Ronald. *Blood Libel, the Damascus Affair of 1840*. New York: Other, 2006.

Franklin, Ruth. *A Thousand Darknesses, Lies and Truth in Holocaust Fiction*. Oxford: Oxford University Press, 2011.

Goldhagen, Daniel Jonah. *The Devil that Never Dies, The Rise and Threat of Global Antisemitism*. New York: Little Brown and Company, 2013.

Gregg, Joan Young. *Devils, Women and Jews, Reflections of the Other in Medieval Sermon Stories*. Albany: State University of New York, 1997.

Gross, Jan Tomasz. *Golden Harvest*. Oxford: Oxford University Press, 2012.

Jacobs, Gerald. *Nine Love Letters*. London: Quartet, 2016.

BIBLIOGRAPHY

Johnson, Paul. *A History of the Jews*. London: Phoenix, 2001.

Julius, Anthony. *Trials of the Diaspora: A History of Anti-Semitism in England*. Oxford: Oxford University Press, 2010.

Kaufmann, Thomas. *Luther's Jews: A Journey Into Anti-Semitism*. Oxford: Oxford University Press, 2017.

Lazare, Bernard. *Antisemitism: Its History and Causes*. Lincoln, NE: University of Nebraska Press, 1995.

Littell, Franklin H. *The Crucifixion of the Jews: the Failure of Christians to Understand the Jewish Experience*. Macon, Georgia: Mercer University Press, 1986.

Luther, Martin. "The Jews and Their Lies." In *Luther's Works, Volume 47: The Christian in Society IV*, 268–293. Philadelphia: Fortress Press, 1971. https://www.jewishvirtuallibrary.org/martin-luther-quot-the-jews-and-their-lies-quot

Maritain, Jacques. *Antisemitism*. London: Centenary, 1939.

Marr, Wilhelm, quoted by Moshe Zimmermann. *Testament of an Antisemite*. Oxford: Oxford University Press, 1986.

Neely, Alan and Winters, Henry Luce. "Oxford 1937: Are They Right?" The Case Study Institute, 2001. New Haven, CT: The Case Clearing House, 2001. https://caseteaching.files.wordpress.com/2011/05/oxford-1937-are-they-right.doc

Nirenberg, David. *Anti-Judaism: the Western Tradition*. New York: Norton, 2013.

Painter, James. *Just James: The Brother of Jesus in History and Tradition*. Edinburgh: T & T Clark, 1999.

Parkes, James. *The Conflict of the Church and the Synagogue*. London: Soncino, 1934.

Plant, Stephen J. "How Theologians Decide: German Theologians on the Eve of Nazi Rule." In *Taking Stock of Bonhoeffer: Studies in Biblical Interpretation and Ethics*, 27–41. Burlington, VT: Ashgate, 2014.

Poliakov, Leon. *The History of Anti-Semitism: Volumes 1–4*. Translated by Richard Howard. New York: Vanguard, 1965–1985.

Rittner, Smith, et al. *The Holocaust and the Christian World: Reflections on the Past, Challenges for the Future*. London: Kuperard, 2000.

Roseman, Mark. *The Villa, The Lake, The Meeting: Wannsee and the Final Solution*. London: Penguin, 2003.

Roth, Cecil. *A Short History of the Jewish People*. London: Macmillan, 1936.

Ruether, Rosemary. *Faith and Fratricide: The Theological Roots of Anti-Semitism*. Eugene, OR: Wipf and Stock, 1997.

Schama, Simon. *The Story of the Jews: Finding the Words, 1000 BCE–1492 CE*. London: Bodley Head, 2013.

Schwarz-Bart, Andre, *The Last of the Just*. London: Secker & Warburg, 1961.

Sebag Montefiore, Simon. *Jerusalem, the Biography*. London: Wiedenfeld & Nicholson, 2011.

Shindler, Colin. *A History of Modern Israel*. Cambridge/New York: Cambridge University Press, 2008.

Shtaynbarg, Eliezer. *The Jewish Book of Fables: Selected Works*. Syracuse: Syracuse University Press, 2003.

Steigman-Gall, Richard. *The Holy Reich: Nazi Conceptions of Christianity. 1919–1945*. Cambridge: Cambridge University Press, 2003.

Stow, Kenneth R. *Alienated Minority: the Jews of Medieval Europe*. Cambridge: Harvard University Press, 1992.

Vermes, Geza. *Jesus in His Jewish Context*. Minneapolis: Fortress, 2003.

Bibliography

Wistrich, Robert. *A Lethal Obsession, Anti-Semitism from Antiquity to the Global Jihad.* New York: Random House, 2010.

Wojdowski, Bogdan. *Bread for the Departed.* Evanston, IL: Northwestern University Press, 1997.

Zimmerman, Moshe. *Wilhelm Marr, the Patriarch of Antisemitism.* Oxford: Oxford University Press, 1986.